FORMATIVE ASSESSMENT STRATEGIES

for Every Classroom

2nd Edition

An ASCD Action Tool

FORMATIVE ASSESSMENT STRATEGIES

for Every Classroom 2nd Edition

 Alexandria, Virginia USA

Susan M. Brookhart

1703 North Beauregard St. • Alexandria, VA 22311-1714 USA
Phone: 1-800-933-2723 or 1-703-578-9600 • Fax: 1-703-575-5400
Web site: www.ascd.org • E-mail: member@ascd.org
Author guidelines: www.ascd.org/write

Gene R. Carter, *Executive Director*; Judy Zimny, *Chief Program Development Officer*, Nancy Modrak, *Publisher*; Genny Ostertag, *Content Development*; Mary Beth Nielsen, *Director, Editorial Services*; Christy Sadler, *Project Manager*; Gary Bloom, *Director, Design and Production Services*; Georgia Park, *Senior Graphic Designer*; Mike Kalyan, *Production Manager*; Valerie Younkin, *Desktop Publishing Specialist*; Carmen Yuhas, *Production Specialist*

PAPERBACK ISBN: 978-1-4166-1083-0   ASCD Product #111005   n07/10

Quantity discounts for the paperback edition only: 10–49 copies, 10%; 50+ copies, 15%; for 1,000 or more copies, call 1-800-933-2723, ext. 5634, or 1-703-575-5634. For desk copies: member@ascd.org.

Library of Congress Cataloging-in-Publication Data
Brookhart, Susan M.
    Formative assessment strategies for every classroom : an ASCD action tool, 2nd ed. / Susan M. Brookhart.—
2nd ed.
        p. cm.
    ISBN 978-1-4166-1083-0 (pbk. : alk. paper)
    1. Teachers—In-service training. 2. Educational tests and measurements. 3. Group work in education.
4. Teachers' workshops. I. Brookhart, Susan M. Exploring formative assessment. II. Title.

    LB1731.B729 2010
    371.26—dc22

                                                                        2010016111

17 16 15   14   13   12   11   10   10 9 7 6 5 4 3 2 1

Formative Assessment Strategies

for Every Classroom—2nd Edition

Section 2: Tools to Use During Direct Instruction

Section 3: Tools to Use During Individual or Group Work on Projects

DOWNLOADS

Electronic versions of the tools are available for download at **www.ascd.org/downloads**.

Enter this unique key code to unlock the files:

G5787-03510-45919

If you have difficulty accessing the files, e-mail webhelp@ascd.org
or call 1-800-933-ASCD for assistance.

ACKNOWLEDGMENTS

Thanks to all the educators and students with whom I am privileged to work, who are a constant source of ideas and encouragement. Thanks to my family—Frank, Carol, and Rachel—for love and support.

Rationale and Planning

What Is Formative Assessment?

Formative assessment refers to the ongoing process students and teachers engage in when they

1. Focus on learning goals.
2. Take stock of where current work is in relation to the goal.
3. Take action to move closer to the goal.

The best formative assessment involves both students and teachers in a recursive process. It starts with the teacher, who models the process for the students. At first, the concept of what good work "looks like" belongs to the teacher. The teacher describes, explains, or demonstrates the concepts or skills to be taught, or assigns student investigations—reading assigned material, locating and reading materials to answer a question, doing activities or experiments—to put content into students' hands. For example, the teacher shares the aspects of a good descriptive paragraph and tells students how their work compares to the ideal. Gradually, students internalize the learning goals and become able to see the target themselves. They begin to be able to decide how close they are to it.

A student's self-assessment process marks the transition to independent learning. When students monitor their own learning and make some of their own decisions about what they need to do next, they are using metacognitive skills. These are important skills in their own right. Learning how to learn—that is, learning the metacognitive skills that will ultimately contribute to lifelong learning—begins with specific acts of self-assessment. Students learn how to monitor their own performance first with respect to specific learning goals they understand; for example, they learn to check sentences for specific comma faults or to check math problems for specific errors. These specific acts of self-assessment during the formative assessment process are critical building blocks as well as strategies for achieving the immediate learning goals. Gradually, students begin to be able to monitor more and more aspects of their work at once.

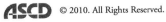

This process is the essence of learning—the continuous process of assessing one's own mastery of content and skills, and discerning and pursuing next steps to move forward toward a goal. The goal may exist only as an objective in a teacher's lesson or unit plan at first, but as students focus on their work, see and monitor their progress, and understand both *what* they are learning and *how* they learn, they become full participants in formative assessment and true learners.

NOT FOR GRADING

Formative assessment is *not* used for grading. Students need—and deserve—an opportunity to learn before they are graded on how well they have learned. Formative assessment is used before instruction, to find out where students are, and during instruction, to find out how they are progressing. The fact that the results of formative assessment are not used for grading makes it even more useful for learning, especially for less-able students. They are free to pay attention to figuring out how they are doing and what they need to work on without worrying about a grade. There is some evidence that good students use all information, including graded work, formatively. This is not the case for students who experience negative feelings after failure. These feelings get in the way of processing additional information about their learning. For such students, the value of feedback is lost, overshadowed by the low grade.

Some experts call assessment before instruction "diagnostic" assessment and reserve the term "formative" for assessment during instruction. Others use "diagnostic" to mean the kind of assessment that, whenever it occurs, gives information to teachers to inform specific lesson plans, the main idea being that diagnostic assessment identifies student weaknesses for teachers to address. Because an important aspect of formative assessment is that both teachers and students use the information, this action tool will use the term "formative assessment" to mean collecting any information, before or during instruction, that can be shared with students and used for improvement.

THE RELATIONSHIP BETWEEN FORMATIVE AND SUMMATIVE ASSESSMENT

Formative and summative assessment should both serve the same learning goals. This is how they are connected. The assessments students use as they develop, practice, and learn should be based on the same knowledge and skills they will ultimately demonstrate for a grade.

Formative assessments give a teacher information about how long to "form" and when to "sum." Some students simply need more practice than others to master knowledge or skills. If formative assessment information says students' work is close to the learning target, those students obviously don't need as much practice and are ready to demonstrate achievement on a summative assessment. Such students can then be given enrichment work related to the learning target or use their time for some other work.

Formative assessment information can come from questioning and discussion with students, from their work (quizzes, assignments, homework), or from direct observation of students doing their work. The tools in this manual are designed to help with this exchange of information by focusing students on aspects of their work and putting those observations on paper where they are easy to see and discuss. When students and teachers routinely share information about the quality of student work relative to the learning targets, learning improves.

In *Understanding by Design,* Wiggins and McTighe (2005) show how formative assessment is an essential part of teaching and learning. They emphasize planning instruction and assessment around desired understandings. These desired understandings are the learning targets that should focus both formative and summative observations.

BENEFITS OF FORMATIVE ASSESSMENT

Research on the use of formative assessment has shown that when teachers practice good formative assessment and students participate in it, both achievement and motivation increase.

The effects of good formative assessment on achievement can be as much as .4 to .7 standard deviations, the equivalent of moving from the 50th percentile to the 65th or 75th percentile on a standardized test. These effects exist at all levels—primary, intermediate, and secondary—and are especially noticeable among lower achievers.

The reasons for these effects are numerous. Formative assessment helps identify what students can do with help and what they can do independently. Participating in formative assessment involves students in active learning, keeps them on task, and focuses them on learning goals. Formative assessment, especially peer evaluation and self-evaluation, helps students with the social construction of knowledge. But more important, formative assessment allows students to receive feedback on precisely what they need to do to improve. It shows them what to do next to get better.

MOTIVATIONAL BENEFITS

The effects of formative assessment on motivation are a little more complicated. Feedback is a message, so the effect depends not only on the information itself but also on the characteristics of the people who send (teachers) and receive (students) the message. One student may hear a helpful, clear description of how to improve a paper with gratitude,

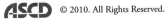

while another may hear the same feedback as just another confirmation of how stupid he is. Covington (1992) talked about "motivational equity," saying that while no two children come to school with equal academic abilities and backgrounds, there is no reason that they should not all have access to equally motivational feedback. The trick is to find out what is motivating for each student. When it's right, it's the best part of teaching and learning. As one teacher said, "To our students it's personal. We are influencing their learning process."

Student self-assessment satisfies both motivational and achievement needs. Students who can size up their work, figure out how close they are to their goal, and plan what they need to do to improve are, in fact, learning as they do that. Carrying out their plans for improvement not only makes their work better but helps them feel in control, and that is motivating. This process, called self-regulation, has been found to be a characteristic of successful, motivated learners.

Student use of formative assessment varies according to students' developmental levels. Younger children can and should participate in evaluating their own work, but they need to be taught how to do that. Research suggests that younger children may focus only on neatness and other surface characteristics of work when they first do self-evaluation. With instruction and practice, however, they learn to focus on the learning target.

Students also have individual differences in their preferences for and use of teacher feedback. Some students may need instruction about how to use feedback and how to do self-assessment. Students who have never experienced self-assessment may at first claim that feedback is solely "the teacher's job." Research suggests, however, that once students realize that information from both teacher feedback and their own self-assessment can help them improve, they will process material more deeply, persist longer, and try harder. In short, they will become more self-regulated learners.

For unsuccessful learners, feedback must deal with negative feelings first, to break the cycle of failure. For these students, formative assessment can help identify specific next steps they can take to do better. Once the students see they are making progress toward achievement, they are more likely to think it is worthwhile to continue. Thus, for unsuccessful students, formative feedback should begin with statements of accomplishment and small, doable steps for improvement.

REFERENCES

Covington, M. V. (1992). *Making the grade: A self-worth perspective on motivation and school reform.* New York: Cambridge University Press.

Wiggins, G., & McTighe, J. (2005). *Understanding by design* (2nd ed.). Alexandria, VA: Association for Supervision and Curriculum Development.

How Does
Formative Assessment Work?

This section describes the formative assessment process as used by successful students and teachers. Recall the three main functions of formative assessment:

1. Focus on learning goals.
2. Take stock of where current work is in relation to the goal.
3. Take action to move closer to the goal.

The chart on the next page reflects these elements. All three are logically connected; for example, students must do something in order to compare their performance with the target performance. The chart describes the formative assessment process from the point of view of both students (left column) and teachers (right column). The student aspect of the process corresponds to the index of student tools in this manual (see pages 18–20) and indicates which tools are appropriate for each stage.

Using the tools will help students participate in the formative assessment process. The tools will also help students share with you information that they might not otherwise communicate during the course of instruction. Use the results of your students' reflections, their expressed understanding of rubrics and criteria, their questions and predictions, and so on, as information to help you understand where they are in their learning. This information will help you focus your instruction.

The formative assessment process is ultimately a communication process between teachers and students. Students need to know what you, the teacher, mean by your assignments and your feedback. You need to understand students' conceptions and misconceptions and their interests, attitudes, and values. The tools in this ASCD Action Tool are designed to help make these communications explicit.

Rationale and Planning

The Formative Assessment Process	
Students	**Teachers**
Understand the target. *(Focus on learning goals.)*	Select and clearly communicate the learning target (understand typical learning progressions in the area).
Produce work.	Make at least one assignment.
Compare the work with the target. *(Take stock of where current work is in relation to the goal.)*	Compare student performance with the desired target or goal, and determine its place in a typical learning progression.
Evaluate strengths and weaknesses.	Evaluate students' strengths and weaknesses.
Prescribe action for improvement.	Give clear oral or written feedback.
Take action for improvement: study, practice, review, rewrite, etc. *(Take action to move closer to the goal.)*	Support or assign action to close the gap.

UNDERSTAND THE LEARNING TARGET

Whether the learning goal is a specific objective for one lesson or a more developmental objective—for example, "become a good writer"—it must be clear to both the teacher and the students. Usually the teacher starts this process by writing or selecting specific learning targets for lessons within the scope and sequence of a district's curriculum, which, in turn, is usually aimed at fulfilling state or professional learning standards. The teacher must clearly understand what constitutes good work and how students' work looks as it progresses toward the goal.

PRODUCE WORK

Once the learning target is clear, the next step is to give students instruction that shares these targets and assignments that call for appropriate work. The more precisely the practice assignments match the learning targets, the more effective they will be—and the more useful they will be for providing formative assessment information to help identify next steps in learning. Section 1 of the Teacher Tools gives some practical strategies for creating classroom assignments and provides some teacher tools.

COMPARE PERFORMANCE WITH THE LEARNING TARGET

This is a skill that needs to be taught! Most students will not automatically reflect on their own work in the manner that you intend. For example, if you ask students, "What did you learn from this activity?" without providing any guidance on how to analyze or evaluate their performance, many will simply copy the title of the assignment: "I learned two-digit subtraction" or "I learned how a bill becomes a law."

Rubrics with clear performance-level descriptions are helpful in this process. Even with good rubrics, however, students need instruction and practice in comparing their work with the description in the rubric. It is helpful, where possible, to have students work together to compare their work to the learning targets, because students are often able to point out qualities in peers' work more easily than in their own. Teachers should provide a "safe" atmosphere for this, so criticism is seen as constructive and part of the learning process. Criticism should not be disparagement. Rather, it should consist of suggestions for improvement, suggestions for how the work could move closer to the goal.

Teachers also add their professional knowledge of learning progressions in the discipline at this point. If you know the common misconceptions your students are likely to have along the way as they learn particular content, you will be able to compare their performance with the ideal more meaningfully and suggest next steps more effectively.

The student tools listed on pages 18–20 will be useful as you instruct students.

EVALUATE STRENGTHS AND WEAKNESSES

Teachers evaluate their observations of student work for several different purposes. First, these evaluations form the basis for feedback to the student (see Teacher Tools, Section 2). Second, they suggest areas for reteaching and review or for enrichment if groups of students share the same strengths and weaknesses.

Students' evaluations of their own work also serve several different purposes. As discussed earlier (see Section 1), evaluating their own work gives students control over their learning, which is motivating. Second, students actually learn by evaluating their own work; a student who sees a weakness is at least beginning to form a concept of what would be better. Third, self-evaluations serve to direct students' further efforts and practice with the learning task at hand.

GIVE FEEDBACK FOR IMPROVEMENT

Teachers' formative feedback to students should be informational, not judgmental. It should include what students need to know to improve. The more specific the feedback is, the better. As a simple example, suppose a student is learning addition facts and takes a timed practice test of 100 facts. The practice test might be returned marked as if for a grade (e.g., 72 out of 100, or 72%). More helpful would be a note with that, saying, "I notice you have more trouble with +7 than with any other facts." Even more helpful

would be that information plus a suggestion on what to do about it: "I notice you have more trouble with +7 than with any other facts. Try making some +7 flash cards and practicing during seatwork time." There should then be time for the student to practice before a test that will be graded.

In *Classroom Instruction That Works,* Marzano, Pickering, and Pollock (2001) review some of the research on the importance of feedback. Section 2 of the Teacher Tools in this action tool describes how to give good feedback and provides some teacher tools for doing so.

CLOSE THE GAP

For formative assessment to truly *form* learning, the gap between the student's performance and the learning goal should become progressively smaller. This may not be a smooth process. Depending on the scope of the learning goal, additional rounds of the formative assessment process may be used. For example, if students write a series of essays in high school, each essay benefits from preceding teacher feedback and self-evaluations. Regardless of the scope of the accomplishment, students should be able to see their work getting closer to the goal, and should understand what specific feedback insights and learning strategies they used to help close the gap. This is an empowering cycle.

REFERENCE

Marzano, R., Pickering, D., & Pollock. J. (2001). *Classroom instruction that works: Research-based strategies for increasing student achievement.* Alexandria, VA: Association for Supervision and Curriculum Development.

Creating Your Own Formative Assessment Tools

As the previous section noted, you should plan for formative assessment as a regular part of your instruction. The indexes in the next section show how to incorporate the student tools in this publication as part of your lesson plans. This section will describe how the tools were constructed so that you can also create your own formative assessment tools.

To create your own formative assessment tools, use four steps:

1. Decide what the purpose of your formative assessment is—that is, which part of the formative assessment cycle you want students to focus on.
2. Select a general formative assessment strategy that will serve this purpose. Five general strategies are described below.
3. Apply the strategy you chose to the particular learning goal you want students to assess.
4. Think about what you will look for as the students use the tool and how you and students will use the information formatively.

SET THE FORMATIVE ASSESSMENT PURPOSE

First, remember that the main purpose of any formative assessment strategy is to engage the student in the formative assessment cycle. As the "Students" side of the chart on page 8 will remind you, this means that any formative assessment tool you design should help students do one or more of the following things. When creating your own formative assessment tool, first identify the tool's purpose from among these steps in the formative assessment process:

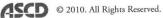

- Understand the learning target.
- Produce work aimed at the learning target.
- Compare the work with the target.
- Evaluate strengths and weaknesses.
- Prescribe action for improvement.
- Take action for improvement (e.g., study, practice, review, rewrite).

SELECT A GENERAL STRATEGY

All of the formative assessment tools in this collection are specific instances of five general strategies: reflection questions, indicator systems, logs or diaries, review of one's own work against criteria, and goal setting or action planning. Almost all formative assessment strategies will fall into one of these general categories. An important point to note is that all of these things require higher-order thinking as students consider their learning targets, their work, or their next steps. For their efforts to be formative—to "form" learning—students must be engaged in actively working out what they should know, what they do know, and what else they need to do.

Reflection questions used at the time an assignment is given might ask students to reflect on their background in, prior experiences with, and attitudes about the topic or skill at hand. Reflection questions can ask students to wonder about a topic or to connect it with other topics they know about. These questions can ask students to identify sticking points or special accomplishments while they are doing an assignment or after they have finished it. The key is that "reflection" means students must grapple with the learning target, their work, and their next steps.

Indicator systems are typically used to help students monitor their understanding during the course of a lesson or class work time. The Happy/Sad tool on page 133 is an example of an indicator. Other common indicator systems include traffic lights (green for "go," red for "stop," yellow for "not sure"), answers to checkup questions displayed on whiteboards, and physical signals (e.g., thumbs up or down).

Logs or diaries can be vehicles for students' planning before work is done or reflection during or after work. The Feedback Request Sheet tool on page 193 is an example of a log-style formative assessment tool used for reflection after students complete their work.

Reviewing students' own work against criteria is commonly done using rubrics or checklists and works best for first drafts of assignments when a revision is possible. The Rubric's Cube tool on page 196 is an example of a formal tool for this. Students can also place rubrics alongside their work and make their own notes on the work or on a separate

Creating Your Own Formative Assessment Tools

sheet of paper without using a formal tool. Your formative assessment strategy in this case would be your plans for helping students learn how to recognize the elements of quality described by the rubrics and to evaluate their own work.

Goal setting and action planning are formative assessment strategies students can use to organize their next steps. Intentional goal setting and action planning will help students focus on the learning target and keep their work organized and on track. Planning tools can help during project work (see the Individual Planner tool on page 172). Goal setting can help students focus on next steps after one round of work is done (see the Goal Setting tool on page 252).

DESIGN THE SPECIFIC STRATEGY

Apply the general strategy you have selected to the specific learning target your students are working on. Here is where your own creativity comes into play. Keeping in mind the needs and abilities of your students, your specific classroom expectations and routines, and especially the formative assessment purpose you want to serve, design the formative assessment tool you will use. For example, write specific reflection questions about identified concepts or skills, design a specific indicator system or form for students to use, and plan the directions or instructions students will need to use the strategy.

DECIDE WHAT TO LOOK FOR

Once you have the specific questions, format, and instructions for a formative assessment tool that will serve your intended purpose, anticipate what students should learn from their own responses to the tool. This step is the easiest to forget, yet also probably the most important. For example, a student can use a rubric to create a brilliant list of insights about his work, but that list is useless unless some action is taken based on these insights.

Build opportunities for students to use the resulting information right into the lesson plans you will use with the formative assessment tool. Students can typically use this information to revise their work, develop detailed plans for what and how to study, make plans for locating additional material or information (e.g., in the library or on the Internet) to use in a project, and so forth. You and your students should not consider that an assessment has happened until there is some sort of related outcome. Then, of course, you and the students should monitor their follow-up and see what happens.

PUTTING IT ALL TOGETHER: CREATING YOUR OWN FORMATIVE ASSESSMENT TOOLS

This section gives two examples of creating your own formative assessment tools using the process outlined above. Though there are only two examples, the possibilities are almost endless.

Example 1: Imagine that you are teaching a unit on recycling. You want to use a formative assessment strategy to help students focus on how they understand the learning target—in this case, what they already know and have experienced about recycling. Understanding the learning target, then, is your purpose. As a general strategy, you decide you will use reflection questions. Specifically, you will design reflection questions about students' background, attitudes, and prior study of recycling.

In this action tool, the example on page 95 (How Did I Get Here?) is designed in a game board format. However, a tool with the same purpose (understanding a learning target about recycling) and general strategy (reflection questions) could use a different design. You might, for example, ask your students to fold paper in half and then in half again, and put questions in each of the "windowpanes" that result:

What interests you about a newspaper recycling project in our town?	Have you ever worked on a recycling project? If so, tell about it.
Do you think recycling newspapers is a good idea? Why or why not?	Have you ever studied recycling in school before?

Or you could use your questions as the basis for a class discussion. If you do, be sure to observe and note student responses that will be useful for future work in the unit. You could also ask groups of four to six students to survey one another and summarize their findings in a chart. You can see here that various different specific designs could all be applications of the general strategy of using reflection questions.

In this example, you are looking for relevant prior experiences: Have any of the students studied recycling before? What did they say they learned? Do any of the students' families recycle, and if so, what kinds of materials? What do these students think about their families' recycling? You and the students could use this information to help select topics for projects in the recycling unit. You could use this information to heterogeneously group students for group work, mixing students who have more and less experience with recycling or more and less positive attitudes toward recycling.

Example 2: Imagine that you are teaching a unit on photosynthesis. You want to use a formative assessment strategy to help students focus on their understanding of photosynthesis concepts during the course of the unit. The general strategy you select is a log or diary entry. Specifically, you will ask students to reflect on what they do and don't understand about photosynthesis. Because quite a few concepts are involved, students will benefit from reflecting on what is clear to them and what still seems confusing. Students put their thoughts into words as they answer questions about their understanding, enabling both you and them to discuss and act on them and to look for points of clarity and of misconception. Students will use those reflections to focus their studying and review, and you will use the same information to plan instruction emphasizing the "neediest" concepts, addressing misconceptions, and acknowledging and building on strengths.

There are many choices for a specific design for this example. The Most and Least Clear tool on page 141 is one such format. You could also ask students to use a page in a classroom journal, if they have one, to answer these questions: What do I understand about photosynthesis? What points are still not clear to me?

Another format suggestion would be to give students 4 x 6" note cards at the end of class, on which they could write exit responses to the above questions. Alternatively, students could note sticking points, write one thing they're sure they know and one thing they're sure they don't, or complete another exercise that would be appropriate for your class setting.

Some teachers use a variation on the exit ticket strategy, asking students to write "entrance tickets." Ask students what is not clear (from yesterday's lesson, last night's homework, or the whole previous unit on photosynthesis, as appropriate) at the start of a class period, and have them write their reflections on sticky notes. Then have them stick the notes on the board, categorizing them as they go by sticking their notes beside ones that are similar. This will result in groups of topics to be addressed and a visual demonstration of the relative need. The bigger the group of notes on any one point, the more students there are who want that point clarified.

What you are looking for here is information on concept understanding and on misconceptions. You will use this information to plan future lessons, spending less time on some concepts and more on others and specifically addressing misconceptions—which you can't do, of course, until you know what misconceptions the students hold. Students will use information from this formative assessment to focus their studying.

GO FOR IT

The point of this section has been to share the strategy used in designing the tools in this resource so that you can create your own formative assessment tools as you need them. These tools are predesigned and thus might save you time. However, the more general aim of this action tool is to help you develop your own capability to use formative assessment strategies and tools for all of the purposes in the formative assessment cycle and for any of your learning targets. If you don't see "just the thing" for your specific formative assessment need in this collection, you can design your own tool to meet your needs.

SECTION 4

Organization of This Action Tool

Whether you design your own formative assessments for students, as explained in the previous section, or you use the student tools provided in this action tool, they should be appropriate for the intended part(s) of the formative assessment process outlined in Section 2. They should also be appropriate for the part of your lesson in which they are used:

- At the time an assignment is given.
- During direct instruction.
- During group or individual work on projects.
- Before summative assessment.
- After summative assessment.

The following pages provide two indexes of the student tools. The first shows which portion of the formative assessment process (as described in Section 2 and listed on each tool's masthead) is involved, as well as which section of the instructional process each tool was designed for. Of course, you can adapt some of the tools for other purposes. Use your understanding of your own students and school setting to make the best use of the tools in your classroom.

The second index helps you identify tools that are helpful for different levels (primary, intermediate, secondary) and for different kinds of class participation (individual, small-group, whole-group). Again, you may adapt the tools for different levels or kinds of participation if you wish.

If you are just starting to experiment with formative assessment, select one or a few things to try. For example, try working with formative assessment at the time an assignment is given, to help students focus on the learning target. As their experience with formative assessment grows, add more opportunities for feedback or student self-assessment during other portions of the learning process.

INDEX OF STUDENT TOOLS AND THE FORMATIVE ASSESSMENT PROCESS							
Formative Assessment Student Tool	Unerstand Target	Produduce Work	Compare Work with Target	Evaluate Strengths and Weaknesses	Prescribe Action for Improvement	Take Action for Improvement	Page Number
Tools to Use When an Assignment Is Given							
Clear Targets	√						71
Sorting Work	√		√	√			75
What's So Good About It?	√		√	√			79
The Rubric Machine	√		√	√			83
The Rubric Translator	√		√	√			87
K-W-L Chart	√		√	√	√		91
How Did I Get Here?	√						95
Crystal Ball	√						98
Riddle Me This	√						101
What Does It Mean to Me?	√		√				105
Planning Sheet	√	√					109
"Pack" for Your Work	√	√					113
Tools to Use During Direct Instruction							
Build from the Blueprint	√	√					119
"Why" Boxes	√	√					123
Spill the Beans		√					126
Circle Around	√	√	√				129
Happy/Sad	√		√	√			133
Up the Ladder	√			√	√		135
The Sticking Point	√	√	√	√			138
Most and Least Clear	√	√	√	√			141
Hit the Target	√			√			145
Huh?	√		√	√	√	√	148
Notes Organizer (1)	√	√					152
Notes Organizer (2)	√	√					155

Rationale and Planning

INDEX OF STUDENT TOOLS AND THE FORMATIVE ASSESSMENT PROCESS (continued)							
Formative Assessment Student Tool	Unerstand Target	Prodduduce Work	Compare Work with Target	Evaluate Strengths and Weaknesses	Prescribe Action for Improvement	Take Action for Improvement	Page Number
Tools to Use During Individual or Group Work on Projects							
Mirror, Mirror	√		√	√	√		161
Me, Me, Me!	√		√	√	√	√	165
Rocket Science	√		√	√	√	√	169
Individual Planner	√	√					172
Group Planner	√	√					175
Action Log	√	√	√				179
Evidence Basket	√		√	√			182
Under the Microscope	√		√	√			186
Conference Call	√		√	√	√		189
Feedback Request Sheet	√	√	√	√	√		193
Rubric's Cube	√		√	√	√	√	196
What Do You Think? What Do I Think?	√		√	√	√	√	199
Peer Review Form	√		√	√	√	√	203
Groupies	√		√	√	√		206
Mission: Possible	√	√					210
Tools to Use Before Summative Assessment							
Minute Math	√	√	√				215
Awesome and On My Way	√		√	√	√	√	218
Cell Phone	√			√	√	√	221
Home Help Sheet	√	√	√	√	√	√	224
T.E.S.T.	√		√	√	√	√	227
"I Get It"	√		√	√	√		230

Rationale and Planning

INDEX OF STUDENT TOOLS AND THE FORMATIVE ASSESSMENT PROCESS (continued)							
Formative Assessment Student Tool	Unerstand Target	Produduce Work	Compare Work with Target	Evaluate Strengths and Weaknesses	Prescribe Action for Improvement	Take Action for Improvement	Page Number
Tools to Use After Summative Assessment							
Do-Overs	√		√	√	√	√	235
Dear Diary	√		√	√	√		239
Progress Map	√		√	√	√	√	243
Strengths and Weaknesses	√		√	√			246
Exercise Program	√				√	√	249
Goal Setting	√				√	√	252
Effort-o-Meter	√		√	√	√		255
Go Over a Test	√		√	√	√		261

INDEX OF STUDENT TOOLS BY LEVEL AND TYPE OF PARTICIPATION							
	Level			Participation*			
Formative Assessment Student Tool	Primary	Intermediate	Secondary	Individual	Small Group	Large Group	Page Number
Tools to Use When an Assignment Is Given							
Clear Targets		√	√	√	√	√	71
Sorting Work		√	√	√	√		75
What's So Good About It?		√	√	√	√		79
The Rubric Machine		√	√		√	√	83
The Rubric Translator		√	√		√	√	87
K-W-L Chart	√	√	√	√			91
How Did I Get Here?		√	√	√			95
Crystal Ball	√	√	√	√	√		98
Riddle Me This	√	√	√	√	√		101
What Does It Mean to Me?		√	√	√	√		105
Planning Sheet		√	√	√	√		109
"Pack" for Your Work	√	√		√	√		113
Tools to Use During Direct Instruction							
Build from the Blueprint		√	√	√	√		119
"Why" Boxes		√	√	√	√		123
Spill the Beans	√	√	√			√	126
Circle Around	√					√	129
Happy/Sad	√			√	√	√	133
Up the Ladder	√	√		√			135
The Sticking Point		√	√	√	√	√	138
Most and Least Clear		√	√	√	√	√	141
Hit the Target	√	√	√	√	√	√	145

INDEX OF STUDENT TOOLS BY LEVEL AND TYPE OF PARTICIPATION (*continued*)							
	Level			Participation*			
Formative Assessment Student Tool	Primary	Intermediate	Secondary	Individual	Small Group	Large Group	Page Number
Tools to Use During Direct Instruction (*continued*)							
Huh?		√	√	√	√		148
Notes Organizer (1)		√	√	√			152
Notes Organizer (2)		√	√	√			155
Tools to Use During Individual or Group Work on Projects							
Mirror, Mirror		√	√	√			161
Me, Me, Me!		√	√	√			165
Rocket Science	√			√			169
Individual Planner		√	√	√			172
Group Planner		√	√		√		175
Action Log		√	√	√	√		179
Evidence Basket	√	√	√	√	√		182
Under the Microscope	√	√	√	√	√	√	186
Conference Call		√	√	√	√		189
Feedback Request Sheet		√	√	√			193
Rubric's Cube		√	√	√	√		196
What Do You Think? What Do I Think?		√	√		√		199
Peer Review Form		√	√		√		203
Groupies		√	√		√		206
Mission: Possible		√	√	√	√		210
Tools to Use Before Summative Assessment							
Minute Math	√	√			√	√	215
Awesome and On My Way		√	√	√		√	218
Cell Phone		√	√	√	√		221

INDEX OF STUDENT TOOLS BY LEVEL AND TYPE OF PARTICIPATION (*continued*)							
	Level			Participation*			
Formative Assessment Student Tool	Primary	Intermediate	Secondary	Individual	Small Group	Large Group	Page Number
Tools to Use Before Summative Assessment (*continued*)							
Home Help Sheet	√	√	√	√			224
T.E.S.T.		√	√	√	√	√	227
"I Get It"		√	√	√			230
Tools to Use After Summative Assessment							
Do-Overs		√	√	√			235
Dear Diary		√	√	√			239
Progress Map		√	√	√			243
Strengths and Weaknesses		√	√	√			246
Exercise Program		√	√	√			249
Goal Setting		√	√	√			252
Effort-o-Meter	√	√	√	√	√	√	255
Go Over a Test		√	√		√		261

*Note: Some individual tools can be adapted for a large group by using the tool with all individuals in a class. Some small-group tools can be adapted for a large group by dividing a whole class into small groups.

ELECTRONIC TOOLS AND RESOURCES

Electronic versions of the tools are available for download. To access these documents, visit www.ascd.org/downloads and enter the key code found on page viii. All files are saved in Adobe Portable Document Format (PDF). The PDF is compatible with both personal computers (PCs) and Macintosh computers. The main menu will let you navigate through the various sections, and you can print individual tools or sections in their entirety. If you are having difficulties downloading or viewing the files, contact webhelp@ascd.org for assistance, or call 1-800-933-ASCD.

Minimum System Requirements

Program: The most current version of the Adobe Reader software is available for free download at www.adobe.com.

PC: Microsoft Windows XP Professional or Home Edition (Service Pack 3 or higher), Windows Vista (Service Pack 1 or higher), or Windows 7, running within the manufacturer's recommended system configuration guidelines. Supported browsers: Internet Explorer 7 (and higher) or Firefox 3.0 (and higher).

Macintosh: Mac OS X v 10.3 or higher, running within the manufacturer's recommended system configuration guidelines. Supported browsers: Safari 3.0 (and higher) or Firefox 3.0 (and higher).

Getting Started

Select "Download files." Designate a location on your computer to save the file. Choose to open the PDF file with your existing version of Adobe Acrobat Reader, or install the newest version of Adobe Acrobat Reader from www.adobe.com. From the Main Menu, select a section by clicking on its title. To view a specific tool, open the Bookmarks tab in the left navigation pane and then click on the title of the tool.

Printing Tools

To print a single tool, select the tool by clicking on its title via the Bookmarks section and the printer icon, or select File then Print. In the Print Range section, select Current Page to print the page on the screen. To print several tools, enter the page range in the "Pages from" field. If you wish to print all of the tools in the section, select All in the Printer Range section and then click OK.

Teacher Tools

Creating Classroom Assignments

Creating classroom assignments that contain clear targets for students is the starting point for both good formative assessment and good instruction. These assignments must be aligned with state standards and curricular goals and must create a learning destination that students can see clearly and plan for.

Good assignments are carefully matched with both the content and the cognitive processes required for learning targets. Content to be learned may include facts, concepts, procedures, or thinking strategies. Cognitive processes required may involve recall, understanding, application, analysis, evaluation, or original creation. If the learning target specifies that a student will be able to use information (e.g., not only understand a weather concept but also use it to predict the weather), then the assignment must call for that.

Good assignments are clearly constructed and have clear directions for students. Good assignments communicate. The student should be able to answer this question: "What am I supposed to do?"

Good assignments tell students the basis on which their work will be evaluated—that is, good assignments share the criteria for quality work. This helps students understand what they are aiming for, and it enables student self-evaluation along the way.

In this ASCD Action Tool, some of the formative assessment tools for students refer to learning targets, but some specifically refer to assignments. For a student, the learning target is made concrete in the assignment. Students will say, "What do you want us to do?" and will mean this as a reference to an assignment. They will think in terms of their work. Therefore, it is critical that your assignments embody your learning targets.

The following three teacher tools are for your use in planning assignments:

Teacher Tools

- Creating Quality Classroom Assignments is a checklist-style planning tool that will help you apply the qualities of good assignments (see previous discussion) as you create or select classroom assignments.

- Blueprint for Pre-assessment gives suggestions for creating a pre-test that is more than a "test" of knowledge. It will also help you plan to pre-assess students' prior experience and attitudes.

- Intervention Framework is a series of three worksheets. If you are sometimes asked to review state or other standardized assessment data and then address deficiencies or differentiate instruction in some way, these worksheets will help you categorize the data and identify areas where you can adapt your teaching appropriately.

Creating Quality Classroom Assignments

STEPS IN THE FORMATIVE ASSESSMENT PROCESS SUPPORTED BY THIS TOOL:

☑ Understand target	❑ Evaluate strengths and weaknesses
❑ Produce work	❑ Prescribe action for improvement
❑ Compare work with target	❑ Take action for improvement

HOW TO USE:

- Identify the learning target or targets.
- Select or construct an assignment that will help students reach that target.
- Use the tool to evaluate the assignment with regard to content match, cognitive process match, clarity, and explicit criteria.

WHAT TO LOOK FOR:

- Assignments are ready to give to students only when you are able to answer *yes* to all questions. Be able to back up your answers with specific evidence from the assignment.

NEXT STEPS:

- If you answer *no* to one of the questions, be able to say exactly what needs to be done to make the answer *yes*. This is trickier than it may seem at first. For example, commenting "Create more higher-order questions" may sound helpful, but you will only accomplish this successfully if you know how to write questions that indeed tap higher-order thinking.
- Use the information to revise your assignment *before* you give it to the students.

TIPS/VARIATIONS:

- For teacher-made assignments, use the tool to help you design and construct your assignments at the outset.

Creating Quality Classroom Assignments   EXAMPLE

Assignment ___Nutrition Diary___

Learning target (objective) ___The student will analyze his or her own eating patterns and assess their nutritional value.___

Qualities of Good Classroom Assignments	Answer Yes or No	Comments: If *yes*, give evidence. If *no*, how will you revise?
Content match with learning target	Does the assignment require the student to use the content specified by the learning target? Yes _X_ No _____	Assignment asks students to list foods eaten for a week and indicate what portion of the food pyramid they're from.
Cognitive process match with learning target	Does the assignment require the student to use the cognitive processes specified by the learning target? Yes _____ No _X_	Objective calls for analysis and evaluation. Need to add analysis (calculate proportion of foods in each section of the pyramid) and evaluation (judge how nutritious their diet is) to the assignment.
Clear to students	Would the student know what to do for all aspects of the assignment? Yes _X_ No _____	Directions are clear. Directions for new parts of the assignment will be similar.
Criteria for evaluation	Are the criteria for evaluating the assignment given, and are they clear? Yes _____ No _X_	Rubrics assess only completeness of food list and categorizing. Add rubrics to assess the analysis and evaluation additions to the assignment.

Creating Quality Classroom Assignments

Assignment _____

Learning target (objective) _____

_____

Qualities of Good Classroom Assignments	Answer *Yes* or *No*	Comments: If *yes*, give evidence. If *no*, how will you revise?
Content match with learning target	Does the assignment require the student to use the content specified by the learning target? Yes _____ No _____	
Cognitive process match with learning target	Does the assignment require the student to use the cognitive processes specified by the learning target? Yes _____ No _____	
Clear to students	Would the student know what to do for all aspects of the assignment? Yes _____ No _____	
Criteria for evaluation	Are the criteria for evaluating the assignment given, and are they clear? Yes _____ No _____	

Teacher Tools

Blueprint for Pre-assessment

STEPS IN THE FORMATIVE ASSESSMENT PROCESS SUPPORTED BY THIS TOOL:

☑ Understand target	❑ Evaluate strengths and weaknesses
❑ Produce work	❑ Prescribe action for improvement
❑ Compare work with target	❑ Take action for improvement

HOW TO USE:

- Identify the learning target or targets.
- Before you teach these learning targets (or this unit), plan to ask questions to understand students' prior knowledge, experience, and attitudes about the subject. Use the tool to plan questions in each domain to ask and discuss with the whole class or individuals or to prompt written answers (not for a grade).
- Ask these questions. Make notes about the group and individuals.

WHAT TO LOOK FOR:

- For the vocabulary and concept knowledge questions, look for level of understanding. Also look for misconceptions that may get in the way of understanding concepts you will be teaching; if you find any, focus instruction to deal with them directly.
- For prior school experiences, attitudes, and personal connections, there are no right or wrong answers. Look for information that will help you understand how your students will approach their work and shape their understandings. You will find both positive and negative experiences, attitudes, and connections, which can provide useful springboards to instruction. It will be important to your students that you seek to understand them and build on that understanding.

NEXT STEPS:

- Use information to adjust instruction. Address misconceptions. When students already know some concepts, build on them instead of merely repeating information.

- Use differences in prior experience and attitudes to form heterogeneous groups for group work.

TIPS/VARIATIONS:

- Use the tool to plan a paper-and-pencil "pre-quiz." Do not grade the quiz, but collect it and review it to help you understand your students.

Creating Classroom Assignments

Blueprint for Pre-assessment

Learning target (objective) _____ Goal: Students will understand plate tectonics._____

Domains for Pre-assessment	Planned Questions	Notes on Responses
Prior school experiences	Have you ever studied plate tectonics before? When? What about volcanoes or earthquakes?	Whole class studied volcanoes in 3rd grade. Armand and Justin have read books about earthquakes.
Vocabulary	Can anyone tell me what these terms mean: sea floor spreading, convection currents, rifts, valleys, trenches, mid-ocean ridges?	Good obvious guesses, but no one has studied scientific definitions for these terms.
Concept knowledge	How do you think continents got their shapes and their locations on the earth?	Trina and Becky both saw the Africa-South America "fit." Once they said it, others did too.
Attitudes	Would you be interested in learning how continents were formed?	Most of the class seems enthusiastic. John and Alissa don't seem interested. Look for ways to engage them.
Personal connections	Has anyone ever been in an earthquake?	Armand used to live in California. He can tell stories about what mild quakes feel like.

Teacher Tools

Creating Classroom Assignments

Blueprint for Pre-assessment

Learning target (objective) _____

Domains for Pre-assessment	Planned Questions	Notes on Responses
Prior school experiences		
Vocabulary		
Concept knowledge		
Attitudes		
Personal connections		

Teacher Tools

⬦ACTION TOOL⬦ Intervention Framework

STEPS IN THE FORMATIVE ASSESSMENT PROCESS SUPPORTED BY THIS TOOL:

☑ Understand target	☑ Evaluate strengths and weaknesses
☐ Produce work	☑ Prescribe action for improvement
☑ Compare work with target	☐ Take action for improvement

HOW TO USE:

- An example of the reading Intervention Framework is presented first, followed by the reading and math Intervention Framework tools. Note that each tool is three pages long.
- Review the results of state or other standardized reading tests for your students. On the basis of those assessment results, identify two areas of instructional concern.
- Identify the next few stories in the basal reading series you are using. On the second page of the tool, indicate where activities used with these stories provide instruction in the identified areas of concern. Circle those that provide direct and explicit instruction.
- On the third page of the tool, use the "Goldilocks" litmus test to identify students for whom that instruction will be "too soft (easy)," "too hard," or "about right." Use these lists to plan differentiated instruction.

WHAT TO LOOK FOR:

- Look for ways that needed remediation, differentiation, and extension of learning targets are already addressed in the curriculum.
- Look for ways to include additional differentiation activities that fold into the scope and sequence you are already accountable for teaching.

NEXT STEPS:

- This tool is organized to plan for differentiated instruction. Carry out the planned interventions, and monitor the results for each student.
- Emphasize the activities listed on page 2 of the tool in your regular teaching—for example, take extra time with these lessons; use all (or most) of the options and

Teacher Tools

Creating Classroom Assignments

additions available to extend these lessons; reinforce these lessons with additional student practice during seatwork, center work, bell work, or other such times; and encourage additional student reflection and discussion on these topics and activities.

TIPS/VARIATIONS:

- Adapt this tool for use with mathematics instruction by replacing the first two pages of the Reading Intervention Framework tool with the mathematics pages (pages 44–45), but using the same third page (the "Goldilocks" page). Review the results of state or other standardized mathematics tests for the students in your classroom. On the basis of the assessment results, identify two areas of instructional concern.

Source: From Beverly A. Long, Armstrong School District, Ford City, Pennsylvania. Used by permission.

Teacher Tools

Intervention Framework

READING

Based on assessment results, identify two areas of instructional concern for your classroom.

Area 1:   **Area 2:**

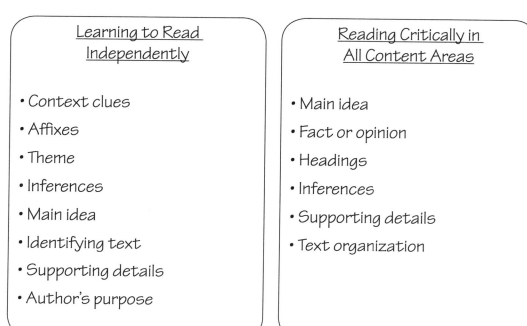

Learning to Read Independently

- Context clues
- Affixes
- Theme
- Inferences
- Main idea
- Identifying text
- Supporting details
- Author's purpose

Reading Critically in All Content Areas

- Main idea
- Fact or opinion
- Headings
- Inferences
- Supporting details
- Text organization

Which stories from the current basal program will you be using for instruction between now and the next assessment point or report period?

1. "Seal Journey"

2. "Do Not Disturb"

3. "Beat the Story Drum"

4. "Kettle of Hawks"

5. "Mom's Best Friend"

6. "Justin and the Best Biscuits"

Teacher Tools

Intervention Framework (*continued*)

 EXAMPLE

Record each instance in which an activity from these basal stories provides direct instruction to support the identified areas of concern.

Area 1:

"Seal Journey"—
Author purpose (pupil's book, p. 38)

"Do Not Disturb"—Context clues (pupil's book, p. 42)

"Beat the Story Drum"

"Kettle of Hawks"

"Mom's Best Friend"

"Justin and the Best Biscuits"—
Point of view (pupil's book, p. 73)

Area 2:

"Seal Journey"

Strategic Reading Main Idea Chart (teacher's guide, p. 122)

Main Idea (pupil's book, p. 37)

Fact or Opinion (teacher's guide, p. 127)

"Do Not Disturb"

Strategic Reading (teacher's guide, p. 142)

Fact or Opinion (pupil's book, p. 44)

"Beat the Story Drum"

"Kettle of Hawks"

"Mom's Best Friend"

Strategic Reading Main Idea Chart (teacher's guide, p. 196)

Main Idea (pupil's book, p. 65)

"Justin and the Best Biscuits"

Circle all activities that provide *direct*, *explicit* instruction.

Teacher Tools

Intervention Framework (*continued*)

Perform the "Goldilocks" litmus test of effective instruction by determining the following:

For which students will the instruction be "too soft (easy)"?

List students by name.

Allie
Tiana
Sarah
Shane S.

How will I differentiate instruction to meet their needs?

- Offer opportunities to be peer tutors.
- Use enrichment activities instead of basic practice for seatwork.

For which students will the instruction be "too hard"?

List students by name.

Cassandra Anthony
Addison   Ansley
Cody   Jordan
Hunter   Shane M.
Kyle

How will I differentiate instruction to meet their needs?

- Reduce assignments.
- Provide extra time.
- Offer opportunities for peer tutoring.

For which students will the instruction be "just right"?

List students by name.

Sierra   *Rikki
Seth   Austin
Zach   Michael T.
Paige   Megan
Keira   Michael F.
Martina

How will I differentiate instruction to meet their needs?

*Make additional observations of Rikki to make sure she is correctly identified in this group.

Intervention Framework

READING

Based on assessment results, identify two areas of instructional concern for your classroom.

Area 1:   **Area 2:**

Which stories from the current basal program will you be using for instruction between now and the next assessment point or report period?

1.   4.

2.   5.

3.   6.

Teacher Tools

Intervention Framework (*continued*)

Record each instance in which an activity from these basal stories provides direct instruction to support the identified areas of concern.

Area 1:

Area 2:

Circle all activities that provide *direct, explicit* instruction.

Teacher Tools

Intervention Framework (*continued*)

Perform the "Goldilocks" litmus test of effective instruction by determining the following:

For which students will the instruction be "too soft (easy)"?

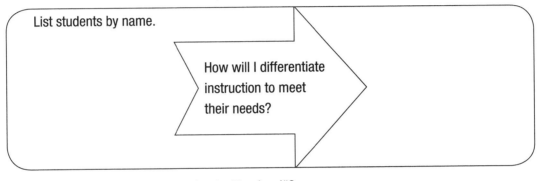

For which students will the instruction be "too hard"?

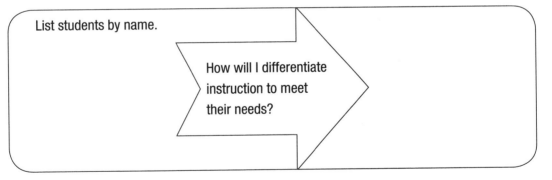

For which students will the instruction be "just right"?

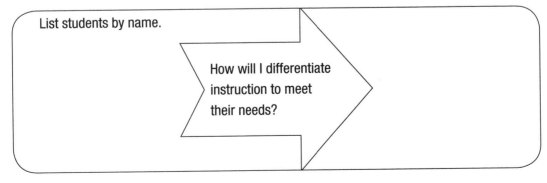

Teacher Tools

☐ 43

Intervention Framework (*continued*)

MATHEMATICS

Based on assessment results, identify two areas of instructional concern for your classroom.

Area 1:   **Area 2:**

What lessons from your current mathematics curriculum or text will you be teaching between now and the next assessment point or report period?

1.   4.

2.   5.

3.   6.

Intervention Framework (*continued*)

Record each instance in which an activity from the math lessons provides direct instruction to support the identified areas of concern.

Area 1:   **Area 2:**

Circle all activities that provide *direct*, *explicit* instruction.

Teacher Tools

Intervention Framework (*continued*)

Perform the "Goldilocks" litmus test of effective instruction by determining the following:

For which students will the instruction be "too soft (easy)"?

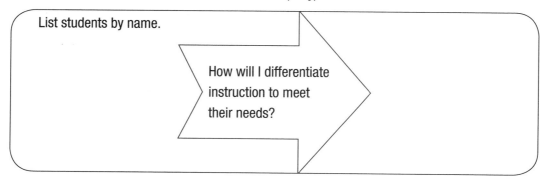

For which students will the instruction be "too hard"?

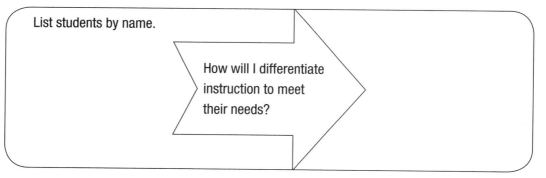

For which students will the instruction be "just right"?

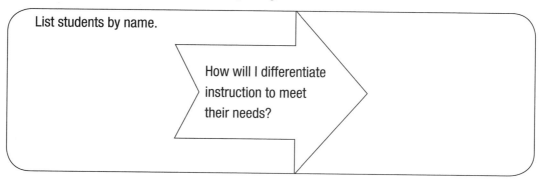

Giving Good Feedback

Good feedback is feedback students both understand and can use to improve. It doesn't matter much whether the feedback sounds good to you, the teacher—if the student can't figure out what to do, it isn't helpful! Research suggests good verbal feedback (oral or written) has the following characteristics.

Good feedback is descriptive, not judgmental. Describe the work, not the student. Use descriptive adjectives. Avoid judgmental words (e.g., "good job," "poor") and instead talk about why the work is good or poor. I-statements (e.g., "I am not sure what you mean here") are better than you-statements (e.g., "You aren't clear").

Good feedback is specific, not general. Use specific vocabulary. Refer to particular aspects of the student's work. Target your remarks to the needs of the particular student, taking into consideration the student's developmental level as well as achievement.

Good feedback is clear to the student. Write simply, avoiding textbook language. Use few pronouns—instead of "this" or "that," use the specific referents.

Good feedback suggests the next steps the student should take to improve. Describe what the next short-term learning goal should be, and suggest specific strategies the student can use to get there.

Teacher tools on the following pages are designed to help you give good feedback. The Feedback Universe is a table describing the different kinds of feedback (e.g., evaluative, descriptive, etc.), the purposes for which each is most suited, and the effects on motivation and learning. Words to Live (and Learn) By is a chart with four principles for giving effective verbal feedback for learning, a good example of each, and a counter-example (what not to do) of each.

Keep records of the important results of formative assessment. Use the data not for grading but to keep yourself organized. For example, you should know what sort of feedback you have given over time to a student on a particular skill (e.g., writing). Three

Teacher Tools

record-keeping sheets (class, individual, and group) are included as tools to help you with that. You can also design your own record-keeping sheets for specific purposes. You may wish to use a computer spreadsheet or database program.

The Feedback Universe

STEPS IN THE FORMATIVE ASSESSMENT PROCESS SUPPORTED BY THIS TOOL:

❑ Understand target	☑ Evaluate strengths and weaknesses
❑ Produce work	☑ Prescribe action for improvement
☑ Compare work with target	❑ Take action for improvement

HOW TO USE:

- This tool is a chart that describes the different kinds of feedback and gives examples. Feedback may be classified as descriptive or judgmental, and as positive or negative. These categories are derived from research.
- Review the tool to understand all the options. Although there are times for all the different types (even harsh words can be appropriate in some situations), the best kind of feedback to support learning is descriptive feedback. Use descriptive feedback as much as possible, and avoid judgmental feedback. Use positive descriptions more than negative descriptions.

WHAT TO LOOK FOR:

- Check that the feedback you give students is descriptive and that the descriptions are statements of how the work relates to criteria you have shared with students.
- Keep in mind that although the intent of descriptive feedback is to give students information they can use to improve, not all students will experience even carefully worded feedback that way. For example, some failing students may simply hear one more reason why they are "stupid," despite your good intentions. Observe how students hear and respond to your feedback and what they do as a result.

NEXT STEPS:

- Provide opportunities for students to use the feedback they receive. Observe the results. Did students benefit from the feedback? In what ways? What still remains to be done?

Teacher Tools

TIPS/VARIATIONS:

- Adapt this tool for students to use when they are giving peer evaluations.

The Feedback Universe

	Positive	Negative
Descriptive	Sharing the criteria for good work. *Example: A good paragraph has a topic sentence and several supporting details that clearly relate to the topic.* Describing the strengths of the work (in terms of the criteria). *Example: Your supporting details are very nice because each of them gives an event from the story that supports your claim that John was ambitious.* Describing what positive actions the student could take to improve. *Example: Work on where to use commas in a sentence, and your next paragraph will be even better.*	Describing the weaknesses of the work (in terms of the criteria). *Example: Your report does not give any more information or insight into the French Revolution than we get from the textbook.* *Example: None of your answers to the word problems are labeled. For instance, you should have written "4 square feet," not just "4."* Describing negative actions that are related to the work. *Example: If you had taken more time and consulted more sources, you would have found additional information for your report.*
	Descriptive feedback is well suited for learning. Giving students information gives them the key and the power to change. Descriptive feedback is also generally motivating. It puts students in control of their work and fosters internal motivation.	
Judgmental	Rewarding the student for good work. *Example: You can have five extra minutes of recess.* Praise that is not linked to work or criteria. *Example: Good for you!*	Punishing the student for poor work. *Example: You stay in from recess today.* Warning or disapproving comments that are not linked to work or criteria. *Example: Watch it, mister!*
	Judgmental feedback leaves students aware of how they are evaluated but does not give them the information they need to do anything about it. Students usually perceive judgmental feedback as controlling. It puts them in the role of working for approval or working to avoid disapproval.	

Words to Live (and Learn) By

STEPS IN THE FORMATIVE ASSESSMENT PROCESS SUPPORTED BY THIS TOOL:

❑ Understand target	☑ Evaluate strengths and weaknesses
❑ Produce work	☑ Prescribe action for improvement
☑ Compare work with target	❑ Take action for improvement

HOW TO USE:

- This tool is a chart that lays out the principles for good verbal (oral or written) feedback. It may be helpful to see the four principles laid out this way, with suggestions and examples. The principles are derived from research.
- This tool is best used for feedback on one assignment to one specific student, but it may also be used as a tool for general reflection on your feedback.
- Review the tool as you prepare to provide feedback to students. Then, give feedback in words that are in keeping with these principles.

WHAT TO LOOK FOR:

- Check your feedback for adherence to the principles. The first page (p. 53) of the tool is a table with some examples of these principles. Then, a checklist version of the tool (p. 54) is provided so that you can evaluate your own feedback.

NEXT STEPS:

- Observe student responses to the feedback. Especially, note whether and in what ways students use your feedback to improve their work.

TIPS/VARIATIONS:

- Use this tool for evaluating (and possibly revising) written feedback you have put on student work.

Words to Live (and Learn) By

How to Give Good Feedback		
Principle: Feedback should	**Suggestions**	**Examples**
Describe and inform (not judge).	Describe the work, not the student.	NOT: *You need to write a better hypothesis.* BETTER: *The hypothesis was too vague to test.*
	Choose adjectives and adverbs that refer to the work.	NOT: *Interesting story!* BETTER: *Freddie is a believable character.*
	Avoid bad judgment words ("poor"); if you use good judgment words, describe what is good.	NOT: *Poor.* BETTER: *Add more details in your summary of Jefferson's theory of democracy.*
	State your own response to the work instead of judging the student.	NOT: *Nice job!* BETTER: *Your story makes me want to meet your uncle.*
		NOT: *You aren't clear.* BETTER: *I can't tell what you mean here.*
Be as specific as possible.	Use specific vocabulary words. Talk about particular aspects of the work.	NOT: *Try harder.* BETTER: *Practice division with remainders.*
Communicate clearly to the student.	Write simply, avoiding "textbook" language. Use nouns instead of pronouns.	NOT: *Not clear.* BETTER: *Your argument that Captain Ahab was crazy doesn't make sense because ....*
Suggest what the student should do to improve.	Describe what the next short-term goal or learning target should be. Suggest a strategy or practice activity that could help the student reach the next goal.	*Your lab report tells all the right facts. Next time, show how those results lead to conclusions about your hypothesis. Find out if there is any recycling going on in your neighborhood. How does that relate to the information in your report? Try making flash cards for your spelling words next week.*

Words to Live (and Learn) By

How to Give Good Feedback		
Principle: Feedback should	**Does my feeback**	**Checklist (add notes, if needed)**
Describe and inform (not judge).	Describe the work, not the student?	Yes _____ No _____
	Choose adjectives and adverbs that refer to the work?	Yes _____ No _____
	Avoid bad judgment words ("poor") or, if I use good judgment words, describe what is good?	Yes _____ No _____
	State my own response to the work instead of judging the student?	Yes _____ No _____
Be as specific as possible.	Use specific vocabulary words?	Yes _____ No _____
	Talk about particular aspects of the work?	Yes _____ No _____
Communicate clearly to the student.	Write simply, avoiding "textbook" language?	Yes _____ No _____
	Use nouns instead of pronouns?	Yes _____ No _____
Suggest what the student should do to improve.	Describe what the next short-term goal or learning target should be?	Yes _____ No _____
	Suggest a strategy or practice activity that could help the student reach the next goal?	Yes _____ No _____

Teacher Tools

Class Observation Tool

STEPS IN THE FORMATIVE ASSESSMENT PROCESS SUPPORTED BY THIS TOOL:

☐ Understand target   ☑ Evaluate strengths and weaknesses

☐ Produce work   ☑ Prescribe action for improvement

☑ Compare work with target   ☐ Take action for improvement

HOW TO USE:

- Use this recording sheet to observe everyone in the class regarding the same or similar behaviors or skills. Put students' names in the first column. Use the remaining columns to note days (or weeks or class periods) and to make notes.
- Use the chart to ensure that you are systematic and include everyone. You will be able to see which students you have observed regarding the target behaviors or skills and make a point to observe the rest of them. For example, a kindergarten teacher might need to make sure she observes each child holding a pencil correctly at least three different times. Or a high school biology teacher might want to observe each student preparing a slide correctly at least two different times. Also, making notes on the chart will result in more complete and organized information than you'd get if you relied on your memory.

WHAT TO LOOK FOR:

- Check to make sure you have had an opportunity to observe all students.
- Look for patterns across rows (students). For example, a student might hold the pencil incorrectly the first three days you are looking, and then begin to hold it correctly. That is a learning pattern. Some patterns may be inconsistent—fine one day, not the next.

NEXT STEPS:

- Use patterns in student performance to plan future lessons.
- Use patterns in student performance as the basis for conversations with students about their learning.

Teacher Tools

TIPS/VARIATIONS:

- Instead of dates across the top, list a different behavior or skill to observe for each column. For example, a kindergarten teacher might list holding pencil, holding scissors, putting away supplies, and so on. Then use the cells in the chart for notes.
- Adapt the tool for talking with students instead of observing them (e.g., assessing interest by asking students what their interests are, and then using the chart to record their answers). The purpose of record keeping is still the same: to ensure that you are systematic and to increase accuracy of information.

Class Observation Tool

EXAMPLE

Class observation for _Used computer workstation properly_

Name	Mon., Sept. 18	Tues., Sept. 19	Wed., Sept. 20	Thurs., Sept. 21	Fri., Sept. 22
Blanton, Amie		Yes		Yes	
Carrington, Bill	Needed help rebooting		Yes		
Cord, Carl		Yes			Helped Bill with shutdown
Jones, Donice	Needed help saving		Yes		
(etc.)					

Teacher Tools

Class Observation Tool

Class observation for _____

Name								

Individual Observation Tool

STEPS IN THE FORMATIVE ASSESSMENT PROCESS SUPPORTED BY THIS TOOL:

❑ Understand target	☑ Evaluate strengths and weaknesses
❑ Produce work	☑ Prescribe action for improvement
☑ Compare work with target	❑ Take action for improvement

HOW TO USE:

- Use this recording sheet to observe one student on several behaviors or skills. In the "Observation" column, list dates. Use the other column headings to name the behaviors or skills you want to observe. For example, a secondary English or language arts teacher might want to observe oral expression, pronunciation, and comprehension. Fill in the chart with notes from your observations about each on a given date. Not every cell needs to be filled.
- Share the information with the student, if appropriate.
- Use the chart to ensure that you are systematic and look for all the behaviors or skills you decided were important. Also, making notes on the chart will result in more complete and organized information than you'd get if you relied on your memory.

WHAT TO LOOK FOR:

- Check to make sure you have had an opportunity to observe each of the things you are looking for. If no natural opportunity has presented itself, you may have to create one.
- Look for patterns. Use the information to draw conclusions about what the student needs.

NEXT STEPS:

- Use patterns in student performance to identify needs for differentiated instruction.
- Use patterns in student performance as the basis for conversations with students about their learning.

Teacher Tools

TIPS/VARIATIONS:

- Put the dates across the top and the behaviors or skills to be observed as the row headings. Use the chart this way to observe the student intensely (over many behaviors or skills) for a shorter time.
- Adapt the tool for talking with, rather than observing, the student. You could use it to record student responses to many things, such as oral questioning on various topics, reading aloud, handwriting, problem solving, and so on.

Individual Observation Tool

EXAMPLE

Student Name *Renee Baptiste*

Observation	On time for class	Has supplies	Works on tasks in groups	Can say what she learned today
Mon., 9/18	√	√	√	√
Tues., 9/19	√	Forgot pencil	(no group)	
Wed., 9/20	10 min. late	√		√
Thurs., 9/21	absent			
Fri., 9/22	√	√	√	√
(etc.)				

Teacher Tools

Individual Observation Tool

Student Name _____

Observation				

Group Observation Tool

STEPS IN THE FORMATIVE ASSESSMENT PROCESS SUPPORTED BY THIS TOOL:

☐ Understand target   ☑ Evaluate strengths and weaknesses

☐ Produce work   ☑ Prescribe action for improvement

☑ Compare work with target   ☐ Take action for improvement

HOW TO USE:

- Use this recording sheet to observe one small group during their group work. You could use it for a short-term group (e.g., a small group working on one project) or a longer-term group (e.g., a reading or math group). List the activities to be observed in the first column (e.g., sharing materials, planning, following directions) and the dates across the top. Write your observation notes in the cells.
- Share the information with the students, if appropriate.
- Use the chart to ensure that you are systematic and look for all the behaviors or skills you decided were important. Also, making notes on the chart will result in more complete and organized information than you'd get if you relied on your memory.

WHAT TO LOOK FOR:

- Check to make sure the group is operating in a manner that will help them accomplish their learning purposes. If they are not, point this out and talk with the students about how to improve.

NEXT STEPS:

- Look for patterns. Use the information to draw conclusions about what the students need. You could also use the information in forming future groups.

TIPS/VARIATIONS:

- Look in the Student Tools section for student group feedback tools. See how the students' perceptions of their work match yours.

Teacher Tools

- Adapt the tool for talking with the group instead of observing them. As you circulate, ask students to comment on their sharing, planning, following directions, and so on. Use the chart to organize your notes as you write them.

Group Observation Tool

Group Members Denise, Katie, LaToya, Marcy

Activities or Focus	Dates			
	10/10	10/12	10/16	10/18
Respectful talking and listening	√	√	Argued loudly—I reminded them about group work expectations	√
All contributing to the work	Katie absent	Katie absent	√	√
Making progress on assignment	√	√	No consensus on how to organize presentation	Still working on how to organize presentation
Getting supplies and putting them away efficiently	√	√	√	√

Teacher Tools

Group Observation Tool

Group Members _____

Activities or Focus	Dates			

Student Tools

Tools to Use ...
When an Assignment Is Given

Tools to Use When an Assignment Is Given

Clear Targets

STEPS IN THE FORMATIVE ASSESSMENT PROCESS SUPPORTED BY THIS TOOL:

☑ Understand target
❑ Produce work
❑ Compare work with target

❑ Evaluate strengths and weaknesses
❑ Prescribe action for improvement
❑ Take action for improvement

HOW TO USE:

- Identify the assignment.
- Ask students to write the assignment directions as given in class on the left side. (For younger children, do this before photocopying.)
- Ask students to write the assignment characteristics they would need to keep in mind to do a good job.

WHAT TO LOOK FOR:

- Look for accuracy, relevance, and completeness:
  - Has the student interpreted the assignment correctly?
  - Are the details the student adds relevant, and would they result in good work on the assignment?
  - Is anything missing from the student's description of what is needed for good work?

NEXT STEPS:

- If necessary, talk with the student about his or her concept of what would constitute good work on this assignment. The purpose is to focus student thinking so the work supports the learning target.
- Have students keep their "target sheet" with them as they complete the assignment and use it for self-assessment. (This supports the "compare work with target" portion of the process.)

Student Tools

TIPS/VARIATIONS:

- Allow students to do this activity in groups instead of individually, which should result in even clearer targets.
- Adapt this activity for primary students by drawing the tool on chart paper. Write and say the assignment (e.g., "Color all the pictures that begin with the *B* sound"), and then write down what the students describe as their ideas of quality work, in storyboard fashion, as the class talks about it.

Clear Targets

EXAMPLE

Assignment ___Book Report on Chapter Book___

What is the assignment?   **What would a good one look like?**

Read a chapter book from the library. Choose any book you want. Show it to Mrs. Brown before you start your report.

Write a two-paragraph book report. First, give a summary of the story. Second, tell what was your favorite part and why.

It would be about an interesting book.

The summary would tell all the important parts of the story in the right order. It would have a beginning, middle, and end. It would name all the main characters.

My favorite part would be the best part. It would talk about the story and me, too.

The report would be neat. My sentences would be good. It would make other people want to read my book.

Student Tools

Clear Targets

Assignment _____

What is the assignment?

What would a good one look like?

Sorting Work

STEPS IN THE FORMATIVE ASSESSMENT PROCESS SUPPORTED BY THIS TOOL:

- ☑ Understand target
- ☐ Produce work
- ☑ Compare work with target
- ☑ Evaluate strengths and weaknesses
- ☐ Prescribe action for improvement
- ☐ Take action for improvement

HOW TO USE:

- Identify an assignment for which you want students to develop understanding of the criteria for good work. In addition to this tool, provide a set of previous students' work that represents a range of quality. Remove the previous students' names, as well as any teacher grades or comments.
- Allow students to do this activity individually, if you wish, but it works best in small groups so that students have a chance to talk about their evaluations of the work.
- Direct the students to sort the work into piles based on their judgment of the quality: high, medium, or low.
- Have students discuss each pile as a set. Ask them to describe the "high" work, the "medium" work, and the "low" work.
- Tell students to use these descriptions to plan how to do their own work on the assignment.

WHAT TO LOOK FOR:

- Observe the descriptions for understanding of the learning target that the assignment was intended to match. For example, some students may think that neatness is more important than substance.

NEXT STEPS:

- If the descriptions adequately describe the intended learning, let students use them for guidance as they work. They may also use them for peer review of one another's work before they turn in their final products.

Student Tools

- If the descriptions do not adequately describe the intended learning, ask students to continue talking about the work they have sorted. Most student groups will be able to arrive at good descriptions eventually, and the process will help them with their learning.

TIPS/VARIATIONS:

- Have students compare and contrast their descriptions of the quality levels with the rubrics that were used to grade the previous students' work. Discussion should focus on the qualities of the work and how important each attribute is. Or you can use these descriptions as the basis for student-generated rubrics.

Sorting Work

EXAMPLE

Assignment ___Current Events Report___

Sort examples of this work into three piles based on quality: high, medium, or low. Look over each pile. In the boxes below, write words that describe each kind of work.

High	Medium	Low
Important event	Pretty important event	Not an important event (maybe picked because it was short)
Clear explanation	Explanation pretty clear	Explanation not well written
Connected to other events or history topics	Reads OK	Sloppy
Easy to read	Fairly interesting	Uninteresting
Neat	News clipping attached	News clipping may not be there
Interesting		
News clipping attached		

Sorting Work

Assignment _____

Sort examples of this work into three piles based on quality: high, medium, or low. Look over each pile. In the boxes below, write words that describe each kind of work.

High	Medium	Low

What's So Good About It?

STEPS IN THE FORMATIVE ASSESSMENT PROCESS SUPPORTED BY THIS TOOL:

☑ Understand target   ☑ Evaluate strengths and weaknesses

❑ Produce work   ❑ Prescribe action for improvement

☑ Compare work with target   ❑ Take action for improvement

HOW TO USE:

- Identify an assignment for which you want students to develop understanding of the criteria for good work. In addition to this tool, provide a set of previous students' high-quality work. Remove the previous students' names, as well as any teacher grades or comments. Note that this tool is similar to Sorting Work (p. 75), except that it focuses only on good work.
- Use this activity individually, if you wish, but it works best in small groups so that students have a chance to talk about their evaluations of the work. Direct students to discuss the question, "What makes this work good?" Tell them to record their answers on the tool.
- Encourage students to use these descriptions to plan how to do their own work on the assignment.

WHAT TO LOOK FOR:

- Observe the descriptions for understanding of the learning target that the assignment was intended to match.

NEXT STEPS:

- If the descriptions adequately describe the intended learning, let students use them for their work.
- If the descriptions do not adequately describe the intended learning, ask students to continue talking about the work they have examined. Most student groups will be able eventually to arrive at good descriptions, and the process will help them with their learning.

      ☐ 79

Student Tools

TIPS/VARIATIONS:

- Suggest that students use these sheets for guidance as they work on the assignment.
- Let students use these sheets for peer review of one another's work before they turn in their final products.

Student Tools

What's So Good About It?

Assignment   _Poetry Analysis_

Select examples of work that you think are especially good. Look at them carefully.

What makes this work good?

The poem is included with the paper so you can read it. The next part tells you what the poem means. It explains the imagery. It discusses the rhyme and meter and word choice. The paper tells why the poem was interesting to read, or it connects the meaning of the poem to a personal experience, or something like that, so the poem seems "real."

What's So Good About It?

Assignment _____

Select examples of work that you think are especially good. Look at them carefully.

What makes this work good?

The Rubric Machine

STEPS IN THE FORMATIVE ASSESSMENT PROCESS SUPPORTED BY THIS TOOL:

☑ Understand target ☑ Evaluate strengths and weaknesses
❑ Produce work ❑ Prescribe action for improvement
☑ Compare work with target ❑ Take action for improvement

HOW TO USE:

- Identify an assignment to focus on. Ask students to identify the qualities of good work on this assignment. They can do this by using the contents of the "High" box from the Sorting Work tool (p. 78) or the comments from the What's So Good About It? tool (p. 82), or they can have a discussion about the qualities of good work as part of their work using this tool.
- Once they have listed the qualities of good work in the "hopper" of the rubric machine, direct students to feed these qualities "through" the machine.
  - For "great" work, tell students to rewrite the qualities exactly as they wrote them in the previous tools or as they agreed during discussion—but instruct them to use rubric language. For example, a quality should be present "clearly" or "completely" to be "great."
  - For "good" work, tell students the language should back down just a bit, so that it describes work that is good but not perfect.
  - For "OK" work, tell students the language should back down another notch. For example, qualities may be "mostly" or only "somewhat" present.
  - For "poor" or unacceptable level work, tell students the language should back down again. Explain that rubrics at this level indicate that few or none of the qualities of good work are present.
- Be aware that students may need help at first with this method of constructing rubrics by backing down from target-quality work. It would be a good idea to go over this process with students the first time they do it. Eventually, students should internalize this kind of thinking and use it as part of their repertoire of study and work skills. Using rubrics will become a strategy they can use for self-evaluation.

Student Tools

WHAT TO LOOK FOR:

- Check that the intended learning target and assignment purpose are reflected in the qualities of good work.
- Check that the rubric's "great" through "poor" categories are reasonable expectations for each of the four levels of quality.
- Check that the same qualities or descriptors are reflected in each of the four levels. For example, if "clear and logical organization" is in the top category, then some description of organization should be in all categories.
- If the rubric needs revision, use the tip below. Have the whole class consider the similarities and differences among each of the small groups' rubrics. The result, with your guidance, should be a rubric suitable for use.

NEXT STEPS:

- Have the students use the rubric for planning their work, for self-evaluation, and for peer evaluation.
- Use the student-generated rubric as your final evaluation tool (for grading). If you are going to do that, tell the students.

TIPS/VARIATIONS:

- Refine the rubric even further by having students compare and contrast the rubrics the small groups developed. Then have them generate one rubric for the whole class to use.

The Rubric Machine

Assignment ___Poetry Analysis___

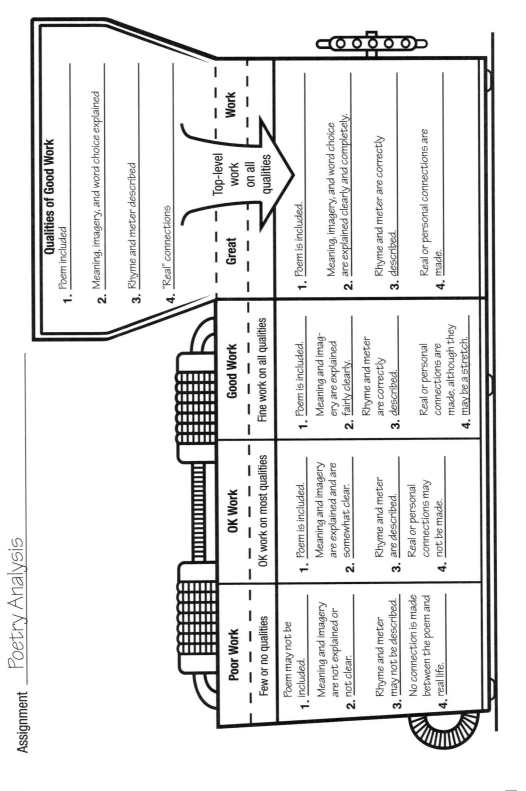

Qualities of Good Work

1. Poem included
2. Meaning, imagery, and word choice explained
3. Rhyme and meter described
4. "Real" connections

Top-level work on all qualities

Great

1. Poem is included.
2. Meaning, imagery, and word choice are explained clearly and completely.
3. Rhyme and meter are correctly described.
4. Real or personal connections are made.

Good Work

Fine work on all qualities

1. Poem is included.
2. Meaning and imagery are explained fairly clearly.
3. Rhyme and meter are correctly described.
4. Real or personal connections are made, although they may be a stretch.

OK Work

OK work on most qualities

1. Poem is included.
2. Meaning and imagery are explained and are somewhat clear.
3. Rhyme and meter are described.
4. Real or personal connections may not be made.

Poor Work

Few or no qualities

1. Poem may not be included.
2. Meaning and imagery are not explained or not clear.
3. Rhyme and meter may not be described.
4. No connection is made between the poem and real life.

☐ 85

Tools to Use When an Assignment Is Given

The Rubric Machine

Assignment _____

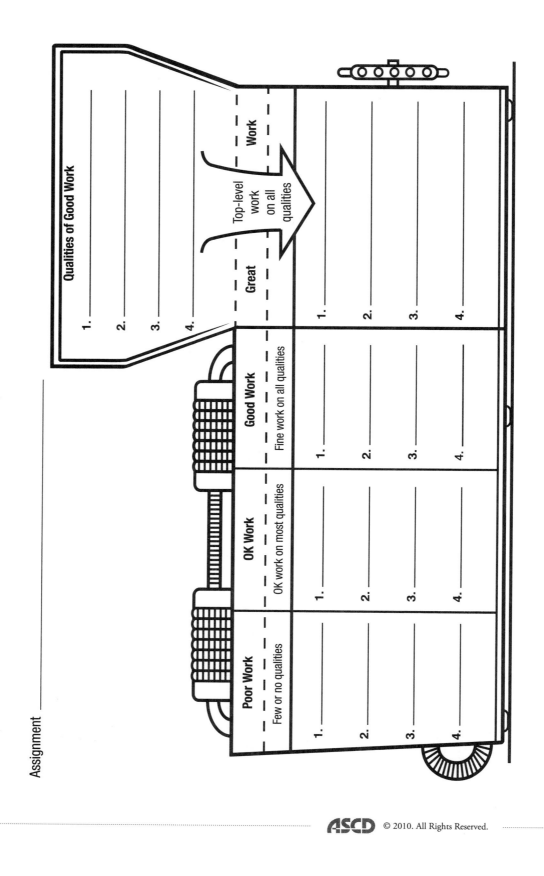

Qualities of Good Work	Great	Good Work	OK Work	Poor Work
	Top-level work on all qualities	Fine work on all qualities	OK work on most qualities	Few or no qualities
1.	1.	1.	1.	1.
2.	2.	2.	2.	2.
3.	3.	3.	3.	3.
4.	4.	4.	4.	4.

The Rubric Translator

STEPS IN THE FORMATIVE ASSESSMENT PROCESS SUPPORTED BY THIS TOOL:

☑ Understand target   ☑ Evaluate strengths and weaknesses
❑ Produce work   ❑ Prescribe action for improvement
☑ Compare work with target   ❑ Take action for improvement

HOW TO USE:

- Select an assignment for which you are going to use a rubric, either your own or a rubric you selected from another source. If the rubric is holistic (one scale for the whole assignment), you can use this tool as is. If the rubric is analytic (several scales—e.g., content, organization, and mechanics for the same assignment), either use this tool for one of the scales you wish students to focus on, or use one sheet for each scale.
- Put the "official" version of the rubric in the top row of boxes, and then photocopy the tool for students. Adapt the tool if the rubric has more than four levels.
- Ask the students to "translate" the description of performance at each level into their own words. Point out that to do this, they will have to consider how to describe the whole range of work, from very good to very poor.

WHAT TO LOOK FOR:

- Check that the student versions of the rubric are accurate and reflect understanding of the levels of performance.

NEXT STEPS:

- Have the students use their translations as guides for their work, for peer evaluation, and for self-evaluation.
- Use the translated rubric to evaluate drafts of work with students before they are turned in. You can do this in several ways: written self-evaluations, written peer evaluations, oral peer evaluations, or brief student-teacher conferences.

Student Tools

TIPS/VARIATIONS:

- Have students work alone to translate the rubric and then get into small groups of three or four to talk about them and decide on a final translation.
- Have students share their translations with the class and use this opportunity to discuss the qualities they—and you—will be looking for.

Student Tools

The Rubric Translator

EXAMPLE

Assignment ___Report on Lewis and Clark___

Teacher Rubric for Content

| The thesis is not clear: Much of the material may be irrelevant to the overall topic or inaccurate. Details are lacking. Appropriate sources were not consulted. | The thesis may be somewhat unclear: Some material and evidence supports the thesis. Some of the material is relevant, and some is not. Details are lacking. Information may include some inaccuracies. At least some sources are appropriate. | The thesis is clear: An adequate amount of material and evidence supports the thesis. Most material is relevant. This material includes details. Information is mostly accurate; any inaccuracies are minor and do not interfere with the points made. Appropriate sources were consulted. | The thesis is clear: A large amount and variety of material and evidence support the thesis. All material is relevant. This material includes details. Information is accurate. Appropriate sources were consulted. |

Student Rubric

| It's hard to find a main idea. I don't have many good facts or references. | My main idea isn't very clear. Facts are sketchy, and I only have a couple good references. | Main idea is clear: I have most of my facts right to support my points, and I have references. | Main idea is clear: I have my facts right to support my points, and I have references. |

The Rubric Translator

Assignment

Teacher Rubric

Student Rubric

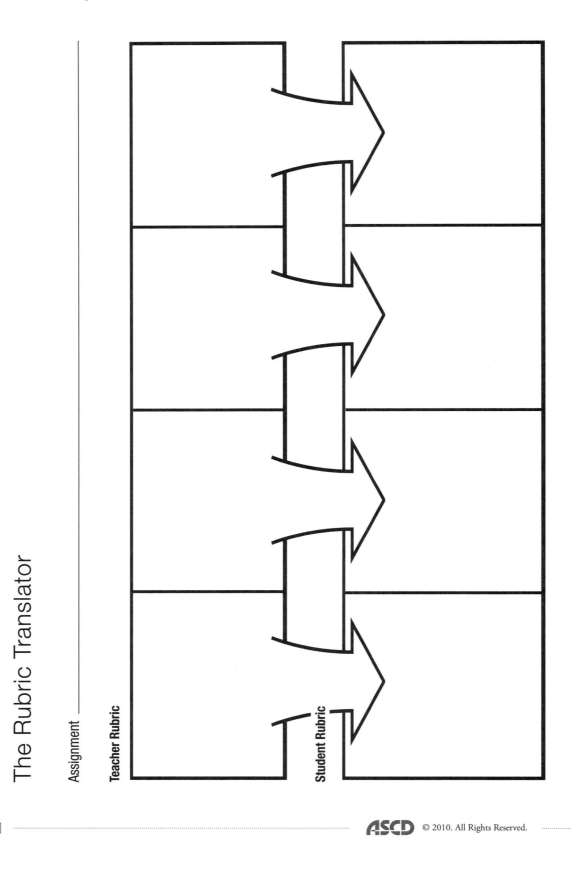

K-W-L Chart

ACTION TOOL

STEPS IN THE FORMATIVE ASSESSMENT PROCESS SUPPORTED BY THIS TOOL:

☑ Understand target
☐ Produce work
☑ Compare work with target

☑ Evaluate strengths and weaknesses
☑ Prescribe action for improvement
☐ Take action for improvement

HOW TO USE:

- Use the K-W-L chart at the beginning of a new unit of study.
- Ask students to fill in what they already know about the topic and what they want to learn about the topic, using the first two columns of the tool. You may start the process by asking those questions as part of a class discussion to stimulate students' thinking.
- At the end of the unit, have students revisit their charts and work on the L column. They should at least answer their W questions. Depending on the nature of the unit, they may also fill in more details about what they learned.

WHAT TO LOOK FOR:

- Observe the K and W columns for relevance to the topic and for level of detail.

NEXT STEPS:

- If a pattern appears (e.g., if most of the class already knows some introductory concepts), adapt instruction so that it becomes a brief review of those concepts, and move on quickly to less-familiar material. Build on what the students know.
- If a few students have in-depth knowledge that others in the class do not have, you may give them enrichment materials, additional reading, and so on. If you use small-group work during the unit, spread the students with in-depth knowledge among the groups to function as more experienced peers and resources.

TIPS/VARIATIONS:

- After they have filled in their own L columns, let students work together in small groups to look at one another's W questions and see if they can add any information to help their peers. This kind of session is useful in its own right, and it can also serve as a study session before a test.
- Have students keep K-W-L charts for a series of units in a folder or notebook and then reflect on a whole report period or other period of learning.

K-W-L Chart

Think about this topic we will study ___The Planets___

What do I **K**now?	What do I **W**ant to know?	What did I **L**earn?
We live on Earth. Earth has land and oceans. Earth has a moon and gravity and air to breathe. I know the names of some other planets: Venus, Mars, and Jupiter.	What are the other planets like? Can people visit other planets? Why are planets there?	[filled in at the end of unit in answer to the W questions]

K-W-L Chart

Think about this topic we will study _____

What do I **K**now?	What do I **W**ant to know?	What did I **L**earn?

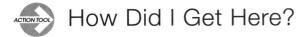 # How Did I Get Here?

STEPS IN THE FORMATIVE ASSESSMENT PROCESS SUPPORTED BY THIS TOOL:

☑ Understand target ☐ Evaluate strengths and weaknesses
☐ Produce work ☐ Prescribe action for improvement
☐ Compare work with target ☐ Take action for improvement

HOW TO USE:

- Tell students that this tool will help activate their prior knowledge through a game board format.
- Identify a learning target or assignment, and put it in the "destination" circle.
- Ask students to reflect on what has gone before, on their own "road" to this destination, and fill in the spaces along the path accordingly.

WHAT TO LOOK FOR:

- Check for relevant experiences students have had and previous school studies they have completed. Plan your instruction to build on those.
- Find out who is interested in which aspects of the topic. For students who do not express interest, look to see whether they had a bad prior experience or simply don't know enough about the topic to be interested.
- For both positive and negative attitudes, ask why and seek to understand the attitude.

NEXT STEPS:

- Use the information to plan differentiated instruction, help students choose appropriate topics for projects or papers, or form heterogeneous groups for group work.

TIPS/VARIATIONS:

- Allow students to keep their "journeys" private or to discuss them with one another.
- Ask students to revisit their interests, attitudes, and experiences after the unit or assignment is finished and tell how they have or have not changed and why.

How Did I Get Here?

Fill in your road.

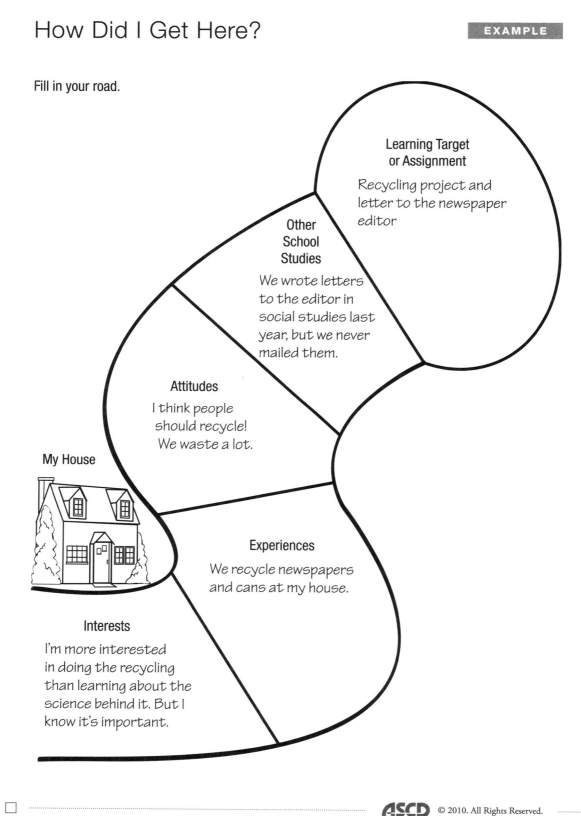

Learning Target or Assignment

Recycling project and letter to the newspaper editor

Other School Studies

We wrote letters to the editor in social studies last year, but we never mailed them.

Attitudes

I think people should recycle! We waste a lot.

My House

Experiences

We recycle newspapers and cans at my house.

Interests

I'm more interested in doing the recycling than learning about the science behind it. But I know it's important.

How Did I Get Here?

Fill in your road.

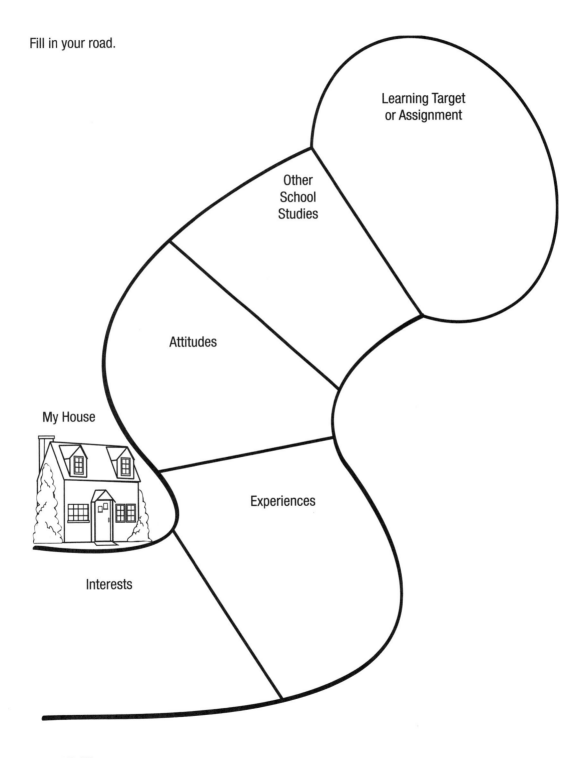

⏻ Crystal Ball

STEPS IN THE FORMATIVE ASSESSMENT PROCESS SUPPORTED BY THIS TOOL:

☑ Understand target	❑ Evaluate strengths and weaknesses
❑ Produce work	❑ Prescribe action for improvement
❑ Compare work with target	❑ Take action for improvement

HOW TO USE:

- Identify a learning target or lesson topic.
- Ask students to predict what they think they will be studying during the lesson or unit. The purpose is to clarify the topic or target and to activate prior knowledge.

WHAT TO LOOK FOR:

- Check that students' predictions are relevant to the topic and show a beginning understanding of the learning target.

NEXT STEPS:

- Refer to students' predictions during instruction as appropriate.
- If predictions are not relevant, use small- or large-group discussions to clarify what the topic does and does not entail. If predictions are relevant but identify facts, concepts, or skills you had not planned to address in your instruction, consider these areas for potential extension or enrichment.

TIPS/VARIATIONS:

- Use this tool for reading fiction (stories or books) by asking students to predict what the story will be about from a title, first paragraph, or first chapter.

Student Tools

Crystal Ball

Learning target or lesson topic ___Community Helpers___

Predict what this will be about. Write your thoughts in the crystal ball.

firefighter

police officer

mayor

playground

ambulance

Crystal Ball

Learning target or lesson topic _____

Predict what this will be about. Write your thoughts in the crystal ball.

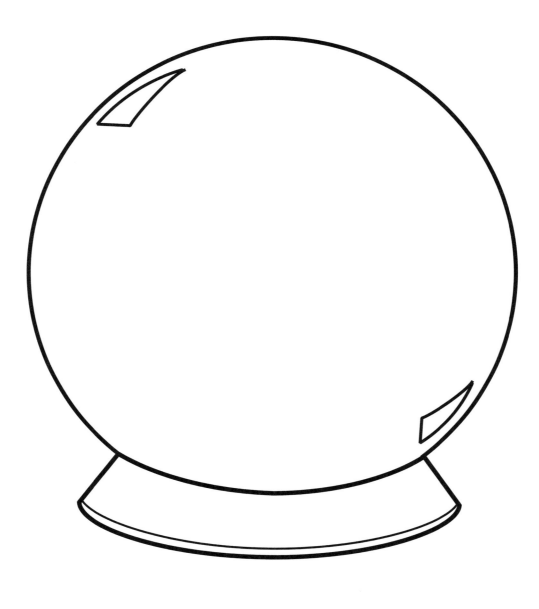

Riddle Me This

STEPS IN THE FORMATIVE ASSESSMENT PROCESS SUPPORTED BY THIS TOOL:

☑ Understand target
❑ Produce work
❑ Compare work with target

❑ Evaluate strengths and weaknesses
❑ Prescribe action for improvement
❑ Take action for improvement

HOW TO USE:

- Identify a learning target or assignment. This tool works well with a textbook reading assignment. It also works well for capturing questions from a series of instructional activities (e.g., a series of science lessons about weather).
- Ask students to reflect on their questions. If you are using the tool with a textbook reading assignment, students can record their questions or points that are still unclear to them after reading. If you are using the tool for a learning target, students can record questions they need to have answered before they will feel they understand or comprehend what is required.

WHAT TO LOOK FOR/NEXT STEPS:

- Look for direct information about what students think they need to know. If their questions are reasonable and clear, help the students answer them directly. This may take the form of providing additional information or additional practice, talking with the students, providing group work that lets students talk with one another, and so on.
- Look for indications of such lack of understanding that students are unable to even ask relevant questions. In this case, remediation is in order.
- Look for students who have no questions about the basic material. Ask these students to note that and then reflect on what else they might want to know.

TIPS/VARIATIONS:

- Use this tool as an individual activity to support students' reflection about what they are supposed to be learning. Used individually, this tool will help you find out what each student's questions are.

- Use this activity in groups. First, have students write their questions individually. Then, in small groups, let students try to answer one another's questions, note the answers to their own questions, and make a group list of any questions left that they couldn't answer together.

Riddle Me This

Learning target or assignment   Math pp. 15–17: Unions, Intersections, and Subsets

Questions about this:

How do you decide whether you need to use a union or an intersection?

Can the same set be both a subset and a union?

Does the U symbol come from the "u" in "union"?

Where can I find some exercises to practice using Venn diagrams?

Riddle Me This

Learning target or assignment _____

Questions about this:

What Does It Mean to Me?

STEPS IN THE FORMATIVE ASSESSMENT PROCESS SUPPORTED BY THIS TOOL:

☑ Understand target	❑ Evaluate strengths and weaknesses
❑ Produce work	❑ Prescribe action for improvement
☑ Compare work with target	❑ Take action for improvement

HOW TO USE:

- Identify an assignment. This tool works well with projects and larger assignments.
- Ask students to reflect and briefly comment on their interest in the assignment; the value and importance it has for them; and the skills, resources, and time they will need to do the assignment.
- Ask students to make explicit their expectations for the work. This gives you a vehicle to see these expectations for each student. Making these things explicit at the outset allows students to get a sense of what it will take for them to do the assignment well. It will allow them to adjust their expectations if necessary.

WHAT TO LOOK FOR:

- Observe and accept students' expressions of interest, value, and importance.
- Observe students' perceptions of the skills, resources, and time needed to complete the assignment.

NEXT STEPS:

- If students express negative feelings, do not "correct" them. That would amount to not accepting their expression of their own feelings. Rather, ask why they feel that way and see if you can learn anything relevant to helping them with the assignment.
- If students' perceptions of needed skills, resources, and time are accurate, you know they are aware of what it would take to succeed. If students' perceptions are not accurate or are incomplete (e.g., if they do not mention an important skill or resource or if they underestimate the time needed), ask them if they can think of anything else.

TIPS/VARIATIONS:

- Have students do this exercise individually, for their own planning and as information for you.
- Allow students to work in small groups, doing the first row (interest, value, importance) individually and the second row (skills, resources, and time needed) together.

What Does It Mean to Me?

Assignment ___Oral History Project___

Fill in the chart to help you see what this assignment means to you.

Interest	Value	Importance
This could be fun because I've never asked my grandma about when she was young.	It will be good to talk with my grandma while she can still tell me this stuff.	I'm not sure how important it is as "real" history, but it will be important to me.
Skills Needed	**Resources Needed**	**Time Needed**
patience writing library	list of good questions newspapers or magazines from the period	1 hr.—interview grandma 2 hrs.—library 2 hrs.—reading 2 hrs.—writing

What Does It Mean to Me?

Assignment _____

Fill in the chart to help you see what this assignment means to you.

Interest	Value	Importance
Skills Needed	**Resources Needed**	**Time Needed**

Planning Sheet

STEPS IN THE FORMATIVE ASSESSMENT PROCESS SUPPORTED BY THIS TOOL:

☑ Understand target ☐ Evaluate strengths and weaknesses
☑ Produce work ☐ Prescribe action for improvement
☐ Compare work with target ☐ Take action for improvement

HOW TO USE:

- Identify an assignment. This tool works well with projects and larger assignments.
- If the project is an individual assignment, have students work individually to plan how they will accomplish the work. If the project is a group assignment, allow students to work in groups to plan it. Ask them to record specific intended steps on the tool. If they need more steps, they can continue on the back of the paper or on additional sheets.
- Avoid having too many tiny steps. The purpose of this tool is for the students to get a sense of the flow of work and for you to see what their sense of the flow of work is.

WHAT TO LOOK FOR:

- Observe that the plans are reasonable and feasible. It will help the students simply to know you are aware of their plans and agree that they are reasonable.
- If an individual student's plans are not reasonable or feasible, talk with the student about them and help the student plan more reasonable steps. If a group's plans are not reasonable or feasible, give them some questions to think about (e.g., How long will it take four of you to do that? How often do you have library time?).

NEXT STEPS:

- Have students keep their planning sheet during their work on the assignment and use it to help them monitor their work.
- Have students evaluate the effectiveness of their plans after the project is completed. What aspects of the plan helped? What might they do differently next time?

TIPS/VARIATIONS:

- As the students plan the work, ask them to add projected dates for accomplishing the steps.

Planning Sheet

Assignment ___Report on the Continental Congress___

My plans for doing this assignment:

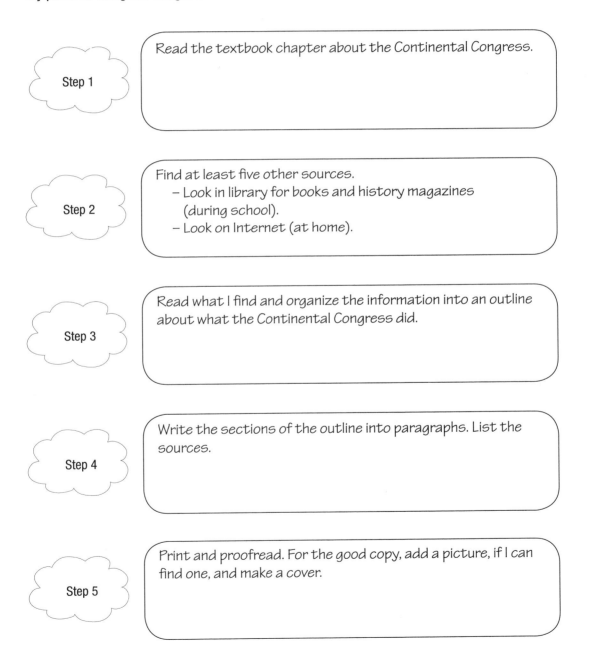

Step 1
Read the textbook chapter about the Continental Congress.

Step 2
Find at least five other sources.
– Look in library for books and history magazines (during school).
– Look on Internet (at home).

Step 3
Read what I find and organize the information into an outline about what the Continental Congress did.

Step 4
Write the sections of the outline into paragraphs. List the sources.

Step 5
Print and proofread. For the good copy, add a picture, if I can find one, and make a cover.

Student Tools

□ 111

Planning Sheet

Assignment _____

My plans for doing this assignment:

Step 1

Step 2

Step 3

Step 4

Step 5

ACTION TOOL "Pack" for Your Work

STEPS IN THE FORMATIVE ASSESSMENT PROCESS SUPPORTED BY THIS TOOL:

☑ Understand target   ❑ Evaluate strengths and weaknesses

☑ Produce work   ❑ Prescribe action for improvement

❑ Compare work with target   ❑ Take action for improvement

HOW TO USE:

- Identify an assignment or project. Ask students to pretend they are going to "pack" their backpacks to do this work. What would they put in? Younger students will list mostly concrete materials. Intermediate-level students may list materials or more abstract things they need (e.g., time), using "packing" more metaphorically.

WHAT TO LOOK FOR:

- Observe the lists for completeness and accuracy. If they are not complete, ask students what else they can think of. If they are not accurate, ask students to explain their choices.

NEXT STEPS:

- Students can use their "pile" of materials as a planning tool for collecting materials and then as a checklist to make sure they have everything.

TIPS/VARIATIONS:

- Allow younger children to color the completed sheet for emphasis, if they wish.

Student Tools

     ❑ 113

"Pack" for Your Work

I need

EXAMPLE

to do Clock Project

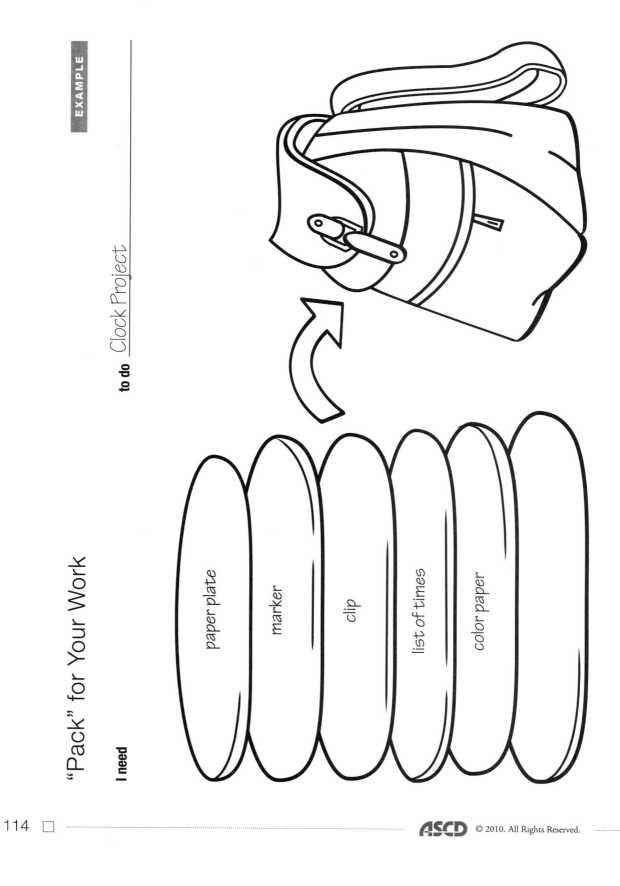

paper plate

marker

clip

list of times

color paper

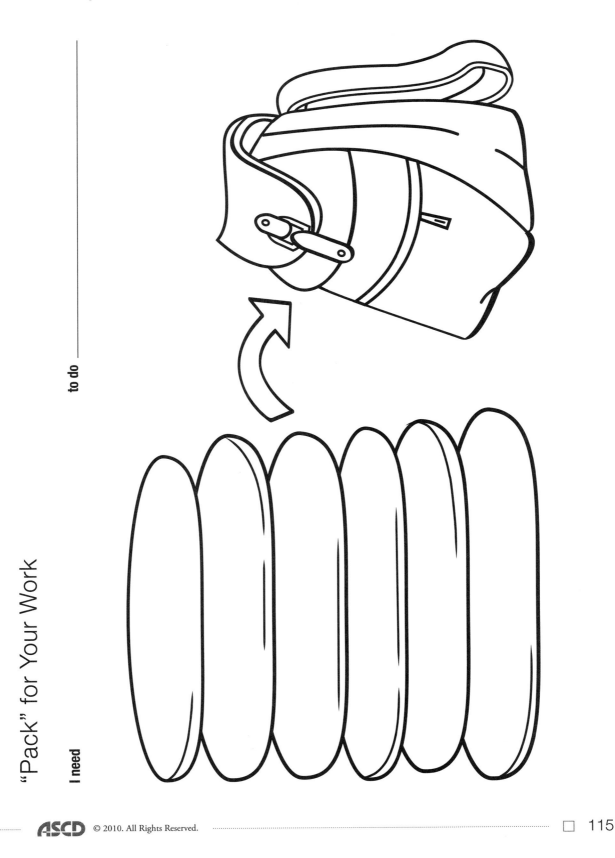

to do

"Pack" for Your Work

I need

Tools to Use ...
During Direct Instruction

Build from the Blueprint

STEPS IN THE FORMATIVE ASSESSMENT PROCESS SUPPORTED BY THIS TOOL:

☑ Understand target	❑ Evaluate strengths and weaknesses
☑ Produce work	❑ Prescribe action for improvement
❑ Compare work with target	❑ Take action for improvement

HOW TO USE:

- In the "Topic" column, list the topics to be covered on an upcoming test or the learning objectives for a unit or part of a unit. Leave the other two columns blank. Copy the tool to distribute to students.
- Ask students to work either individually or in small groups to write practice questions—one fact question and one reasoning question—for each topic. You may need to give examples of fact and reasoning questions and discuss the difference.

WHAT TO LOOK FOR:

- Check that the students' questions match the topic and intended learning objectives. Revise, or have students revise, questions that do not match.
- Check to make sure that the students' questions require knowledge of facts or reasoning, as intended.
- Look at the content of the questions for information about what students understand about the topic. Aspects of a topic that are missing may indicate areas students did not understand. (Students have to know something in order to write a good question.)

NEXT STEPS:

- Have students use the tool to quiz each other in small groups.
- Collect the students' questions and use them to construct a practice test (or several) for students to use when they are studying.
- Have students play review games using questions from the tool.

Student Tools

TIPS/VARIATIONS:

- Have students explain their reasoning questions.
- Make this a regular activity. Get students in the habit of writing questions as a way to consolidate their understanding. Use throughout a unit (e.g., after each main topic), and then compile the results to help students study for the unit test.

Build from the Blueprint

A test blueprint is a plan for making a test. It lists topics your next test will cover. Write two practice questions for each topic: one fact question and one reasoning question.

Test name ___Moon___

Topic	Fact Question	Reasoning Question
moon's structure	What is the moon's crust made of?	Explain why scientists think the moon may have an iron core.
moon's surface	What are the "maria" on the moon?	Why do the surfaces of the near and far sides of the moon look different?
orbit and moon phases	How long does it take the moon to orbit Earth?	Show how the moon comes to look like a crescent.
tides	What causes the tides?	If the moon is over New York City, where will high tides be?

Build from the Blueprint

A test blueprint is a plan for making a test. It lists topics your next test will cover. Write two practice questions for each topic: one fact question and one reasoning question.

Test name _____

Topic	Fact Question	Reasoning Question

Student Tools

"Why" Boxes

STEPS IN THE FORMATIVE ASSESSMENT PROCESS SUPPORTED BY THIS TOOL:

☑ Understand target   ❑ Evaluate strengths and weaknesses

☑ Produce work   ❑ Prescribe action for improvement

❑ Compare work with target ❑ Take action for improvement

HOW TO USE:

- Use science or math problems that require reasoning and lend themselves to students' showing their work. You can fill them in before copying, or you can use blank sheets so students can do different problems.
- Ask students to solve the problem, showing all steps, and explain their reasoning in the boxes.
- Teach students how to write explanations, if necessary, to help them get started.

WHAT TO LOOK FOR:

- Check work for quality of reasoning, completeness, and accuracy.
- Check to see that students' reasoning matches the work in each step.
- If there is more than one way to solve a problem, accept any reasonable path to the solution.

NEXT STEPS:

- Having students write their reasoning will make it visible so that you can identify any misconceptions or skipped steps. Use this diagnostic information to plan further instruction.

TIPS/VARIATIONS:

- Allow students to work in small groups to review one another's reasoning.

Student Tools

"Why" Boxes

Solve the problem below and show your work. Explain why you took each step.

Problem

Mr. Smith's classroom is 20 feet wide and 30 feet long. He wants to put 12-inch-deep bookshelves on three walls—the two short walls and one of the long ones. He wants to figure out how much floor space he would have left. What is the area the bookshelves would take, and what is the area left for floor space?

Solution

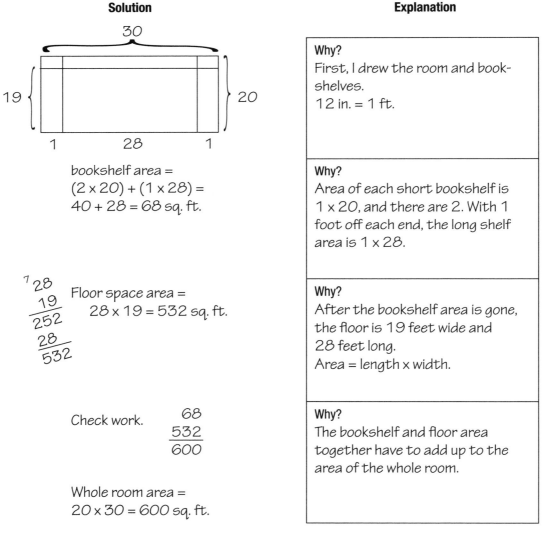

bookshelf area =
$(2 \times 20) + (1 \times 28) =$
$40 + 28 = 68$ sq. ft.

$$\begin{array}{r} {}^{7}28 \\ 19 \\ \hline 252 \\ 28 \\ \hline 532 \end{array}$$

Floor space area =
$28 \times 19 = 532$ sq. ft.

Check work.
$$\begin{array}{r} 68 \\ 532 \\ \hline 600 \end{array}$$

Whole room area =
$20 \times 30 = 600$ sq. ft.

Explanation

Why?
First, I drew the room and book-shelves.
12 in. = 1 ft.

Why?
Area of each short bookshelf is 1 x 20, and there are 2. With 1 foot off each end, the long shelf area is 1 x 28.

Why?
After the bookshelf area is gone, the floor is 19 feet wide and 28 feet long.
Area = length x width.

Why?
The bookshelf and floor area together have to add up to the area of the whole room.

Tools to Use During Direct Instruction

"Why" Boxes

Solve the problem below and show your work. Explain why you took each step.

Problem

Solution	Explanation

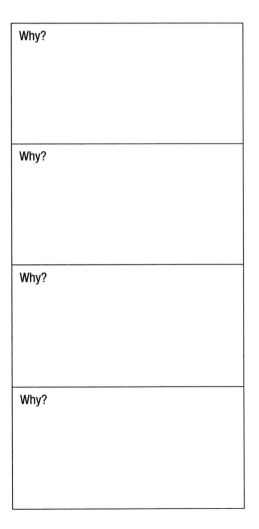

Spill the Beans

ACTION TOOL

STEPS IN THE FORMATIVE ASSESSMENT PROCESS SUPPORTED BY THIS TOOL:

❑ Understand target	❑ Evaluate strengths and weaknesses
☑ Produce work	❑ Prescribe action for improvement
❑ Compare work with target	❑ Take action for improvement

HOW TO USE:

- Use this tool to ensure randomness in calling on students, giving each student an equal chance at participating in class. For some kinds of classroom discussions or lessons, this helps students stay engaged.
- Write each student's name on a sheet of paper and cut so each name appears on a single strip. Distribute the strips to the students. Ask students to roll the strips into a round shape and place them in a container (a can or basket).
- Shake up the container of "beans" and then draw one or spill one out. Call on the person whose name is selected.

WHAT TO LOOK FOR:

- Observe the class to see whether the random calling creates an atmosphere in which all students stay more engaged than if they participated in discussion only on a volunteer basis.

NEXT STEPS:

- Look for other ways to create a "learning atmosphere" (as opposed to a grading or judgmental atmosphere) in your classroom. Create and support an atmosphere in which mistakes are opportunities for learning and everyone's voice is valued.

TIPS/VARIATIONS:

- Use this tool when you can reasonably expect that most students should have something to say if asked. Do not use it when introducing new or difficult material or in other situations where random calling might seem like a trap.

Spill the Beans

Write each student's name on a strip of paper. Distribute the strips to the students. Have the students roll their strip into a "bean" and put it in a can. Shake the can of "beans" and spill one or more as needed to select students to respond to classroom questions.

Roy Ames	Allison Barber
Sarah Collier	Alan Coyne
Melinda Elder	Aidan Frist
Brandon Hatch	Carlos Martinez
(and so on)	

Spill the Beans

Write each student's name on a strip of paper. Distribute the strips to the students. Have the students roll their strip into a "bean" and put it in a can. Shake the can of "beans" and spill one or more as needed to select students to respond to classroom questions.

Circle Around

STEPS IN THE FORMATIVE ASSESSMENT PROCESS SUPPORTED BY THIS TOOL:

☑ Understand target
☑ Produce work
☑ Compare work with target

☐ Evaluate strengths and weaknesses
☐ Prescribe action for improvement
☐ Take action for improvement

HOW TO USE:

- This game-style activity allows children to practice asking questions of one another. Use the tool to prepare and distribute to the class a set of questions for a topic or lesson review.
- Have all students stand. Divide the class into two equal-size groups. In case of an odd number of children, ask one to stand out to help you, and then rotate that child in after a few rounds.
- Tell each group to arrange themselves in a circle, one inside the other. Instruct the inside circle to walk clockwise and the outside circle to walk counterclockwise, until you call time. Vary the amount of time (as in the game "musical chairs") so students cannot predict when you will stop them.
- When you call time, have students in the inside circle and outside circle face each other. This results in sets of partners. Have the "inside" students ask their "outside" partner one of the questions. Then reverse, having "outside" students ask their "inside" partner a question.
- If you wish, ask, "Who got an especially good answer?" and invite that student to share his or her answer.
- After this exchange, direct the student circles to move again and repeat the process.

WHAT TO LOOK FOR:

- Listen for individual student needs and for patterns of group understanding and misunderstanding.
- Listen for good peer evaluation. Students should check one another's answers and give helpful suggestions if needed.

 Student Tools

NEXT STEPS:

- If you hear particular misconceptions, use this diagnostic information to plan further instruction.
- Work on students' question-writing skills.

TIPS/VARIATIONS:

- Use this activity with younger children, especially when they have been seated for a while and need to move.
- Have students work in small groups to prepare the list of questions used in this activity.

Circle Around

Questions

1. What is a fable?

2. Why did Tortoise win the race?

3. Who was your favorite—Tortoise or Hare?

4. What does "the moral of the story" mean?

5. What was the moral of this story?

6. Why was Hare faster?

7. When you run, are you like Tortoise or like Hare? Why?

8.

9.

Circle Around

Questions

1.

2.

3.

4.

5.

6.

7.

8.

9.

Happy/Sad

STEPS IN THE FORMATIVE ASSESSMENT PROCESS SUPPORTED BY THIS TOOL:

☑ Understand target   ☑ Evaluate strengths and weaknesses
☐ Produce work   ☐ Prescribe action for improvement
☑ Compare work with target   ☐ Take action for improvement

HOW TO USE:

- Tell children to draw and color a happy face on the front of the circle. Then, have them cut it out, turn it over and color the back side as a sad face.
- Direct children to put the circle on the corner of their desk and use it as an indicator. Explain that "happy side up" means they understand the lesson and what they are supposed to be doing, and that "sad side up" means confusion, misunderstanding, "I'm stuck," and the like.
- Use this activity for two reasons: (1) to create an easy way to see students' understanding and (2) to teach children to do ongoing self-evaluation.

WHAT TO LOOK FOR:

- Monitor class understanding at a glance by looking across desks.

NEXT STEPS:

- Adjust instruction, directions, or level of help for individuals or groups as needed.
- Ask students to explain why they turned up their sad face before you try to help. Use their own understanding as a starting point.

TIPS/VARIATIONS:

- With older students, use a variation on this activity for written work they turn in. Provide sheets of happy- and sad-face stickers, or just sheets of red- and green-circle stickers. Have students evaluate their own work before they turn it in. If they are happy with the work, tell them to affix a happy face or green-circle sticker. If they would like help or extra feedback because they want to do better, tell them to affix a sad face or red-circle sticker. Provide extra written feedback or conferencing for students whose stickers indicate a need for it.

Student Tools

Happy/Sad

Draw and color a happy face. Cut it out. Draw and color a sad face on the back.

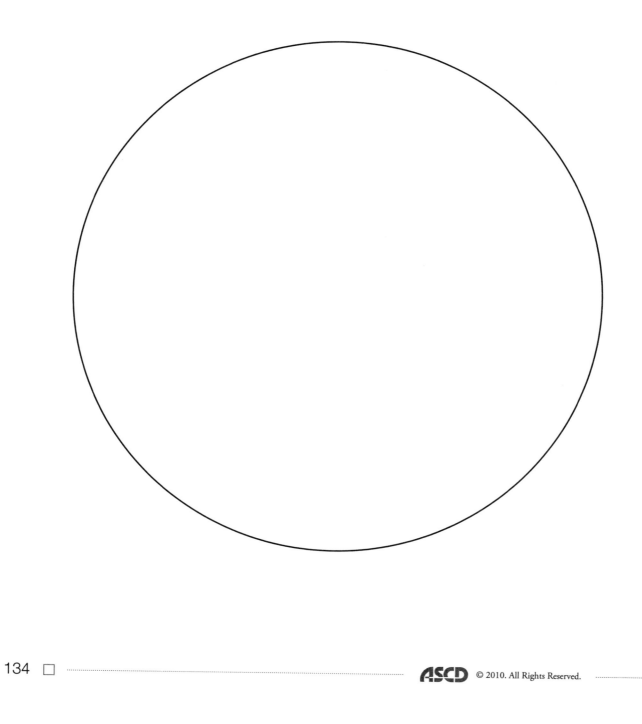

Up the Ladder

STEPS IN THE FORMATIVE ASSESSMENT PROCESS SUPPORTED BY THIS TOOL:

☑ Understand target ☑ Evaluate strengths and weaknesses

❑ Produce work ☑ Prescribe action for improvement

❑ Compare work with target ❑ Take action for improvement

HOW TO USE:

- Use this tool with a short-term goal that has identifiable parts.
- Identify the parts that "climb" the ladder, from the most basic step at the bottom to the most complex step at the top. Write these in for younger students before you duplicate the sheet. Older students can write the steps themselves.
- Younger students can draw a stick figure on the appropriate rung to represent themselves as they progress. Older students can color in the appropriate rung or use the list like a checklist.

WHAT TO LOOK FOR:

- Look for accurate student appraisal of their progress.

NEXT STEPS:

- Have students use the list of progress steps to help them decide what to work on next.

TIPS/VARIATIONS:

- Use regularly for short-term goals that are repeated—for example, mastery of spelling units or sets of vocabulary words in a content area.

Student Tools

Up the Ladder

My progress toward _Spelling Unit 4 Mastery_

I can use each word correctly in my regular everyday writing.

I can use each word correctly in a sentence.

I know the definitions of all the words and can spell them.

I can spell all the words.

Tools to Use During Direct Instruction

Up the Ladder

My progress toward _____

_____

_____

_____

_____

The Sticking Point

STEPS IN THE FORMATIVE ASSESSMENT PROCESS SUPPORTED BY THIS TOOL:

☑ Understand target   ☑ Evaluate strengths and weaknesses

☑ Produce work   ❑ Prescribe action for improvement

☑ Compare work with target   ❑ Take action for improvement

HOW TO USE:

- Identify a learning target or assignment.
- Ask students to reflect on and describe where they get stuck in the material. For some subjects, this would be a description of concepts the students don't understand. For other subjects, it might be a description of a skill or skills students need to practice.

WHAT TO LOOK FOR:

- Check the students' comments and note where the sticking points are.
- Check that the reflections are accurate. Some students may need help to learn how to evaluate their own understandings and figure out what they know and don't know.

NEXT STEPS:

- Use the information you gather for individual remediation, for adjusting group instruction, or for deciding what to emphasize or what next steps to take with the material.

TIPS/VARIATIONS:

- Recognize that students may need practice to be able to describe what they don't know. Time spent teaching this skill is time well spent, because it will help students be able to ask for help more clearly and effectively, and thus will allow you to get them the help they need more easily.

The Sticking Point

Learning target or assignment ___Factoring Quadratic Equations___

Here is where I get stuck:

I have trouble seeing how to find factors. I can go from factors to expanded notation. I can do

$$(2x - y)(x + 2y) = 2x^2 - xy + 4y - 2y^2 =$$

$$2x^2 + 3y - 2y^2$$

but if you just gave me this

I can't go the other way and factor. I'd be like—how do you get a 3 out of those 2s? I don't see it.

The Sticking Point

Learning target or assignment _____

Here is where I get stuck:

Most and Least Clear

STEPS IN THE FORMATIVE ASSESSMENT PROCESS SUPPORTED BY THIS TOOL:

☑ Understand target ☑ Evaluate strengths and weaknesses

☑ Produce work ☐ Prescribe action for improvement

☑ Compare work with target ☐ Take action for improvement

HOW TO USE:

- Identify a learning target or assignment.
- Ask students to reflect on what is most and least clear in the material and to write their comments in the appropriate boxes. In some subject areas, students would describe concepts they do and don't understand. In other subject areas, students might describe skills in which they do or don't need more practice.
- Note that this tool is similar to The Sticking Point (p. 138) except that it focuses on both the positive and negative.

WHAT TO LOOK FOR:

- Check the students' written reflections and note what the clear and unclear aspects are.
- Check that the reflections are accurate. Some students may need help to learn how to evaluate their own understandings and figure out what they know and don't know.

NEXT STEPS:

- Use the information you gather for individual remediation, for adjusting group instruction, or for deciding what to emphasize or what next steps to take with the material.
- Where possible, help students see connections between their own efforts and their understandings. For example, aspects a student finds most clear may be aspects the student worked on carefully. Enabling students to see clear connections between effort and achievement or understanding helps foster students' desire for mastery of their schoolwork.

Student Tools

TIPS/VARIATIONS:

- Recognize that students may need practice to be able to describe what they don't know. Time spent teaching this skill is time well spent, because it will help students be able to ask for help more clearly and effectively, and thus will allow you to get them the help they need more easily. It will also enable them to see connections between their effort and understanding more easily.

Most and Least Clear

Learning target or assignment __Moon—read chapter and answer questions__

These points were most clear to me.

Definitions:
- crust, mantle, and core
- terrae, maria, and craters

Facts (like distance)

Moon orbit, phases, dark and light sides

Theories of the moon's origin

These points were least clear to me.

How the moon's gravity causes tides

When tides are low and high (how to figure that)

Most and Least Clear

Learning target or assignment _____

These points were **most clear** to me.	These points were **least clear** to me.

Hit the Target

STEPS IN THE FORMATIVE ASSESSMENT PROCESS SUPPORTED BY THIS TOOL:

☑ Understand target   ☑ Evaluate strengths and weaknesses
❑ Produce work   ❑ Prescribe action for improvement
❑ Compare work with target ❑ Take action for improvement

HOW TO USE:

- Use this tool with a quantifiable short-term goal—where progress can be measured with quiz scores, for example. To be truly formative, use the target with practice quizzes, where progress made can be reflected in a final grade later on.

- You may choose to label the target rings. If you use a standards-based report card, you might label the rings with levels matching your standards of progress: for example, Beginning, Basic, Proficient, and Advanced. In other settings you might use a percent band: for example, 0–50, 51–75, 76–90, 91–100. Be sure that these "scores" are for students' information, not for final grading. Progress won't be reflected in the final grade if beginning practice scores are included in the grade average.

- Students keep track of their "hits" so that their chart will eventually look like an archery target.

WHAT TO LOOK FOR:

- Look for students' accurate appraisal of their progress.

NEXT STEPS:

- Have students use the target to inform their studying and to celebrate their success.

TIPS/VARIATIONS:

- Use regularly for short-term goals that are repeated: for example, mastery of spelling units, math facts, or types of math problems.

 □ 145

Hit the Target

Look at your work on _graphing linear functions_

Place a dot on the target and the date you made that "hit."

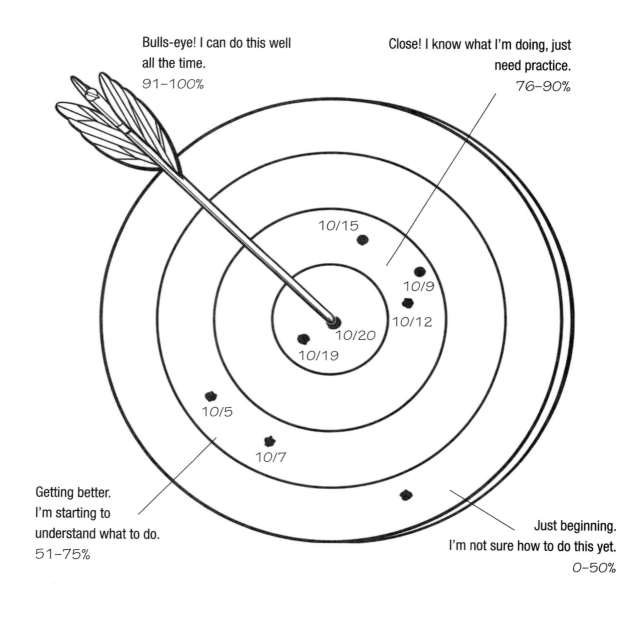

Bulls-eye! I can do this well all the time.
91–100%

Close! I know what I'm doing, just need practice.
76–90%

10/15

10/9

10/12

10/20

10/19

10/5

10/7

Getting better. I'm starting to understand what to do.
51–75%

Just beginning. I'm not sure how to do this yet.
0–50%

Hit the Target

Look at your work on _____

Place a dot on the target and the date you made that "hit."

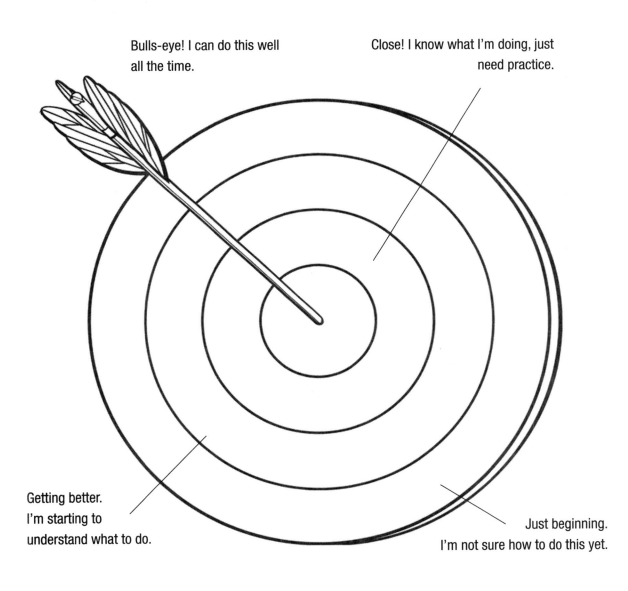

Bulls-eye! I can do this well all the time.

Close! I know what I'm doing, just need practice.

Getting better. I'm starting to understand what to do.

Just beginning. I'm not sure how to do this yet.

ACTION TOOL Huh?

STEPS IN THE FORMATIVE ASSESSMENT PROCESS SUPPORTED BY THIS TOOL:

☑ Understand target
❑ Produce work
☑ Compare work with target

☑ Evaluate strengths and weaknesses
☑ Prescribe action for improvement
☑ Take action for improvement

HOW TO USE:

- Identify a reading assignment that students have already read.
- Ask students to reflect on what they learned from the passage and to identify aspects of the reading that they feel are still unclear.

WHAT TO LOOK FOR:

- Check students' reflections for level of understanding. Are they focusing on memorizing facts or on developing conceptual understanding? Does their focus match the purpose of the assignment?
- Observe whether students feel empowered by learning how to improve their own comprehension. Point out that developing skills to check for their own understanding—and then doing something about it—are important for lifelong learning.

NEXT STEPS:

- Have students use their completed sheet of reflections as an advance organizer for rereading the assignment. During their rereading, they can take notes beside the points and topics they identified as unclear.
- Check for evidence of improvement after focused rereading. If you do not see improvement, try to determine why: inaccurate student self-reflection, a text that is too difficult, inadequate background knowledge, and so on. Each reason should suggest a different avenue for remediation.

Student Tools

TIPS/VARIATIONS:

- Allow students to work in groups instead of individually. The group should discuss what is not clear to all of them. They should then reread the passage and report back about whether they can shed any more light on their questions. If they are still confused, suggest that they search for information in another source—another textbook, an encyclopedia, and so on.

☐ 149

Huh?

Huh?

I just read Investigating Science, pages 30–35

Here are three things I didn't understand completely:

(1) molecules

_____

The part I didn't understand was How do atoms stick

together?

_____

(2) elements

_____

The part I didn't understand was What's the difference

between an element and an atom?

_____

(3) compounds

_____

The part I didn't understand was How do they get that

way (compounded)?

Reread the assignment.
Use this page as a bookmark. Take notes on your three topics.

Notes

Huh?

Huh?

I just read _____

Here are three things I didn't understand completely:

(1) _____

_____

The part I didn't understand was _____

_____

(2) _____

_____

The part I didn't understand was _____

_____

(3) _____

_____

The part I didn't understand was _____

_____

Reread the assignment.
Use this page as a bookmark. Take notes on your three topics.

Notes

 # Notes Organizer (1)

STEPS IN THE FORMATIVE ASSESSMENT PROCESS SUPPORTED BY THIS TOOL:

☑ Understand target   ❑ Evaluate strengths and weaknesses
☑ Produce work   ❑ Prescribe action for improvement
❑ Compare work with target   ❑ Take action for improvement

HOW TO USE:

- Use this tool to help students organize their notes from a reading passage. Identify the reading assignment, then have students use the template to organize their notes by main idea.
- Use Notes Organizer (1) for passages with several main ideas of more or less equal weight. Use Notes Organizer (2) (p. 155) for passages with one main conceptual framework.

WHAT TO LOOK FOR:

- Check that the students have selected important main ideas and given relevant supporting details. These are reading comprehension skills.

NEXT STEPS:

- If the notes are of good quality, students can use them as study aids.
- If students do not identify important main ideas and relevant supporting details, probe to find out why. It could be that the text is too difficult or that they have inadequate background knowledge.

TIPS/VARIATIONS:

- Give students time to get used to organizing their notes and to internalize the strategy. Eventually, they should not need a tool to take organized notes.

Notes Organizer (1)

EXAMPLE

Notes on ___Viruses___

Main idea #1
Viruses are active only inside living cells. Outside a cell, viruses are dormant.

Details
- structure: protein coat over DNA or RNA
- hooks to receptor site in cell membrane, injects DNA or RNA
- hijacks the cell function

Main idea #2
The body has defenses to keep viruses from attaching.

Details
- skin
- natural antiseptics for openings (saliva, tears, mucus, stomach acid)

Main idea #3
When viruses get through the defenses and attack, the immune system starts to work.

Details
- B cells make antibodies.
- Microphages surround the viruses.
- T cells send messages.

☐ 153

Student Tools

Notes Organizer (1)

Notes on _____

Main idea #1

Details

Main idea #2

Details

Main idea #3

Details

Notes Organizer (2)

ACTION TOOL

STEPS IN THE FORMATIVE ASSESSMENT PROCESS SUPPORTED BY THIS TOOL:

☑ Understand target   ❑ Evaluate strengths and weaknesses

☑ Produce work   ❑ Prescribe action for improvement

❑ Compare work with target   ❑ Take action for improvement

HOW TO USE:

- Use this tool to help students organize their notes from a reading passage. Identify the reading assignment, then have students use the template to organize their notes as a summary and supporting points.
- Use Notes Organizer (1) (p. 152) for passages with several main ideas of more or less equal weight. Use Notes Organizer (2) for passages with one main conceptual framework.

WHAT TO LOOK FOR:

- Check that the students have summarized important main ideas as a meaningful whole and have given relevant supporting details. These are reading comprehension skills.

NEXT STEPS:

- If the notes are of good quality, students can use them as study aids.
- If students have not summarized important main ideas as a meaningful whole and have not given relevant supporting details, probe to find out why. It could be that the text is too difficult or that the students have inadequate background knowledge.

TIPS/VARIATIONS:

- Give students time to get used to organizing their notes and to internalize the strategy. Eventually, they should not need a tool to take organized notes.

Student Tools

EXAMPLE

Notes Organizer (2)

Notes on ___Light___

Summary of Main Ideas

Light is a special form of
electromagnetic radiation.
Light is a form of energy.
Properties of light allow us
to see objects and effects.

Supporting Points

rays—straight lines
shadows—umbra and penumbra
transparent, translucent, opaque (light through, partly
   through, or stopped/reflected)
mirrors reflect light rays
refraction—bending light
    water
    glasses
    lenses
   periscopes
   telescopes
   glasses
   microscopes
   magnifying glasses
   cameras

Notes Organizer (2)

Notes on _____

Summary of Main Ideas

Supporting Points

Tools to Use ...
During Individual or Group
Work on Projects

Mirror, Mirror

ACTION TOOL

STEPS IN THE FORMATIVE ASSESSMENT PROCESS SUPPORTED BY THIS TOOL:

☑ Understand target   ☑ Evaluate strengths and weaknesses
❑ Produce work   ☑ Prescribe action for improvement
☑ Compare work with target   ❑ Take action for improvement

HOW TO USE:

- Use this tool for students' self-evaluation and revision before work is turned in.
- Give students a copy of the assignment directions and rubric for reference. The purpose of listing the criteria on the mirror is to focus attention; students will not be able to write an entire rubric in that space.
- Ask students to look over their work with the criteria for the assignment in mind. Have them write constructive criticism in the reflection box. That information will help students see what needs to be revised for their final draft.

WHAT TO LOOK FOR:

- Check that the evaluations and criticisms are relevant (based on the criteria and assignment directions), accurate, and complete.

NEXT STEPS:

- If a criticism is unfounded or inaccurate, ask the student why he or she made that comment. If the evaluation is incomplete, ask the student about the criterion that was omitted. Make sure evaluations are relevant, accurate, and complete before students use them to revise their work.
- If you wish, review the self-reflections before the students use them for revisions. You may use the sheets as a vehicle for brief student-teacher conferences about their work on the assignment.

Student Tools

TIPS/VARIATIONS:

- The mirror metaphor implies student self-evaluation. If you adapt the tool for peer evaluation, remind the students that peers may make suggestions but the final word on what and how to revise rests with the students themselves. If students do not agree with an evaluation a peer makes, they can ask for an explanation of the criticism to help them decide how to respond to it.

Student Tools

Mirror, Mirror

Look at your work on _The George Washington Report_

What do you see?

I have good information. There is more content than I need, but I want to leave it all in because it's interesting—especially the stuff about Washington as a general.

I organized the report by time, but I don't think that's clear the way I wrote it. I will make sure each paragraph starts with a topic sentence that includes a date or time. I could add some section titles, too.

The spelling and punctuation are good. It reads a little choppy (like my stuff always does!). I'll try to make it smoother.

I need to check the bibliography format.

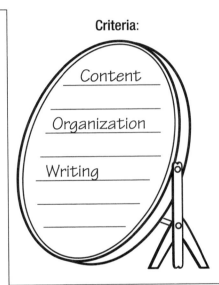

Criteria:

Content

Organization

Writing

Mirror, Mirror

Look at your work on _____

What do you see?

Criteria:

Me, Me, Me!

STEPS IN THE FORMATIVE ASSESSMENT PROCESS SUPPORTED BY THIS TOOL:

☑ Understand target   ☑ Evaluate strengths and weaknesses

☐ Produce work   ☑ Prescribe action for improvement

☑ Compare work with target   ☑ Take action for improvement

HOW TO USE:

- Use this tool when a project is in the beginning stages. The purpose is for the students to identify where they will need to focus their efforts. Ideally, the students will see that these portions of the work are within their control, will be amenable to effort (possibly with help), and will expect success.
- Ask the students to reflect, individually, on what the assignment entails and to identify three things that will require the most effort. Then have the students apply the three survey-style questions to each point they identified, reflecting on their likelihood of success and whether they will need help.

WHAT TO LOOK FOR:

- Check the identified areas for relevance and importance. Are they things that are needed for the assignment, and are they integral to its success? Students need not list everything required for the assignment, just the three aspects that they think will be most difficult for them.
- Look at the survey questions. The questions have no right or wrong answers. The purpose is to elicit the students' perceptions. Making their thoughts explicit may be sufficient for some students to see what to do about them, but other students may need help to address the aspects of the assignment they identified.

NEXT STEPS:

- If students say they are "not very likely" to succeed on a particular element, ask why. Help those students plan how to increase their likelihood of success. Then, check to see that any planned sources of help (survey question b) are appropriate.

Student Tools

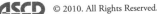

TIPS/VARIATIONS:

- Use this tool as an individual worksheet. Students should get in the habit of asking these kinds of questions for all assignments and asking for appropriate help as needed.

Student Tools

Me, Me, Me!

EXAMPLE

Assignment _Poetry_

For this assignment, list the three things you need to work on most. Answer the questions for each one.

1. finding *good poems to use*	a. Can I do this myself? ● Yes ○ No b. If no, who could help? ○ Teacher ○ Other student _____ ○ Family member _____ c. How likely am I to succeed? ○ Not very ○ Possibly ● Likely
2. writing my own poem on the same themes	a. Can I do this myself? ○ Yes ● No b. If no, who could help? ○ Teacher ● Other student _Sarah_____ ○ Family member _____ c. How likely am I to succeed? ○ Not very ● Possibly ○ Likely
3. explaining how my poem is like the classic poem	a. Can I do this myself? ● Yes ○ No b. If no, who could help? ○ Teacher ○ Other student _____ ○ Family member _____ c. How likely am I to succeed? ○ Not very ○ Possibly ● Likely

Me, Me, Me!

Assignment _____

For this assignment, list the three things you need to work on most. Answer the questions for each one.

1.	a. Can I do this myself? ○ Yes ○ No b. If no, who could help? ○ Teacher ○ Other student _____ ○ Family member _____ c. How likely am I to succeed? ○ Not very ○ Possibly ○ Likely
2.	a. Can I do this myself? ○ Yes ○ No b. If no, who could help? ○ Teacher ○ Other student _____ ○ Family member _____ c. How likely am I to succeed? ○ Not very ○ Possibly ○ Likely
3.	a. Can I do this myself? ○ Yes ○ No b. If no, who could help? ○ Teacher ○ Other student _____ ○ Family member _____ c. How likely am I to succeed? ○ Not very ○ Possibly ○ Likely

Rocket Science

STEPS IN THE FORMATIVE ASSESSMENT PROCESS SUPPORTED BY THIS TOOL:

☑ Understand target
☐ Produce work
☑ Compare work with target

☑ Evaluate strengths and weaknesses
☑ Prescribe action for improvement
☑ Take action for improvement

HOW TO USE:

- Use this tool to give younger students a concrete reminder of actions they need to take for improvement, based on feedback you and each individual student agree on.
- On the moon, write the topic or skill you and the student agree needs improvement.
- Ask the student to identify strategies he or she will use. The student can write the strategies on the rocket, or you can write them as the student dictates.
- Let the students keep the tool on their desks as a reminder to carry out the strategies.

WHAT TO LOOK FOR:

- Be sure that the area (topic or skill) identified for the student to work on is important but focused enough that the student will see short-term improvement.
- Check that the strategies the student identifies are appropriate and effective, and that they are within the student's capabilities.

NEXT STEPS:

- Have students use the strategies during class work on the topic or skill.
- When you and the student are satisfied that the strategies have led to improvement, write comments to that effect on the sheet and let the student take it home. The more specific the comments are, the better. For example, "You can now do all of the 7+ and 8+ facts correctly" is more helpful than "Nice job, Amanda!"

TIPS/VARIATIONS:

- Let students color the sheet, if they wish, and use it as a cover sheet for work.

Rocket Science

EXAMPLE

Rocket Science for _Amanda_

I need to

Learn 7+ and 8+ facts

How I will get there

flash cards every day

draw pictures

practice quiz

Tools to Use During Individual or Group Work on Projects

Rocket Science

Rocket Science for _____

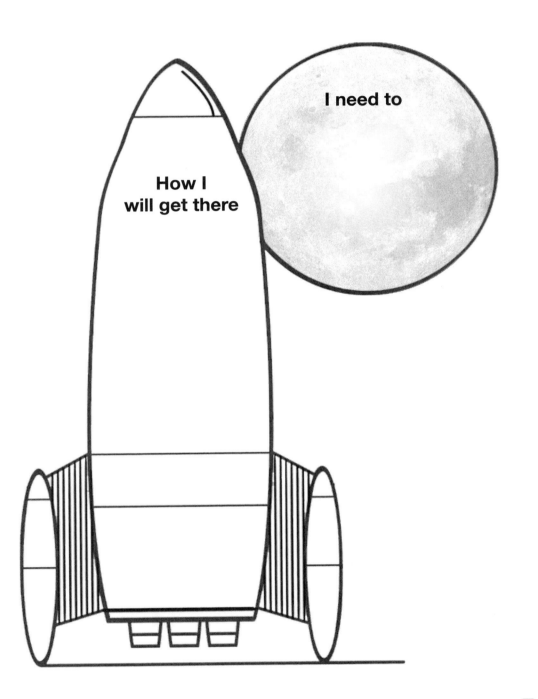

Student Tools

Individual Planner

ACTION TOOL

STEPS IN THE FORMATIVE ASSESSMENT PROCESS SUPPORTED BY THIS TOOL:

☑ Understand target	❑ Evaluate strengths and weaknesses
☑ Produce work	❑ Prescribe action for improvement
❑ Compare work with target	❑ Take action for improvement

HOW TO USE:

- Use this tool to help students construct a plan for work on a long-term individual project. In the first column, have students list all separate tasks involved in the project. Then show them how to use the chart as a visual organizer to plan when they will work on each task. They can simply color in the days to make a bar chart, or they can make more detailed notes for each day (as in the example).
- Have students keep the chart with them and use it to do their work.

WHAT TO LOOK FOR:

- Check that the task list is accurate and complete. Check that the time allotted in the students' plans is reasonable. Any order of tasks that will result in a completed project is acceptable. Different students may structure their plans differently; time estimates should be reasonable for the individual.
- If students leave out a critical task, or under- or overestimate time, talk with them about the plans. Ask them to think some more about the project, why they think a task will take a certain amount of time, and so on.

NEXT STEPS:

- Monitor students' use of their planners.
- After the project is completed, ask students to reflect on how useful their plans were and how they could make them more useful next time. Learning to plan work is an important skill.

TIPS/VARIATIONS:

- Allow students to revise their time estimates during the course of the week. Some students will want to "check off" things they have done.

Student Tools

Individual Planner

EXAMPLE

Plan for work on ___Report on the Bronze Age—research phase___

Tasks	Monday	Tuesday	Wednesday	Thursday	Friday		
Look up information	Library during class	Library after school	Library if needed				
Use Internet	Use Internet at home, get articles			← Get pictures for report →			
Read material, take notes		← Read what I get from library and Internet →					
Organize material				← Sort information into categories for outline →			

Individual Planner

Plan for work on _____

Tasks	Monday	Tuesday	Wednesday	Thursday	Friday

Group Planner

STEPS IN THE FORMATIVE ASSESSMENT PROCESS SUPPORTED BY THIS TOOL:

☑ Understand target   ❑ Evaluate strengths and weaknesses
☑ Produce work   ❑ Prescribe action for improvement
❑ Compare work with target   ❑ Take action for improvement

HOW TO USE:

- Use this tool to help students construct a plan for work on a long-term group project. Have students list group members' names in the first column. Next have them list the tasks to be accomplished, in order, in the top row. Tell students to use the chart as a visual organizer to plan their work.
- Have students keep the chart with them as they do their work.

WHAT TO LOOK FOR:

- Check that the task list is accurate and complete. Different groups may structure their plans differently.

NEXT STEPS:

- Check that all individuals participate and that tasks assigned to individual students are reasonable.
- If a group leaves out a critical task, ask them what else they might have to do for the project.
- For some kinds of group work, assign all or some of the individuals' roles and responsibilities. The Group Planner can be used in this case, but check to make sure that students have planned in accordance with their assigned roles.
- After the project is completed, ask students to reflect on how useful their plans were and how they could make them more useful next time. Learning to plan work is an important skill.

Student Tools

TIPS/VARIATIONS:

- Allow group members to verify that the division of responsibilities is fair—that is, that all members have approximately equivalent amounts of time and effort. Help them to consider approximately equal opportunities for learning, too. Some students will want to "check off" things they have done.

Student Tools

Group Planner

Plan for work on _Report on the Bronze Age_

EXAMPLE

Name	Research—look up	Write summary—share with group	Read and review	Read and review	Final production
Jordan	Bronze Age in the Near East	→	Bronze Age in Asia (Shaun's summary)	Bronze Age in Europe (from Carlos and Shaun)	Word processing and bibliography
Carlos	Bronze Age in Europe	→	Bronze Age in Near East (Jordan's summary)	Bronze Age in Asia (from Shaun and Jordan)	Time line
Shaun	Bronze Age in Asia	→	Bronze Age in Europe (Carlos's summary)	Bronze Age in the Near East (from Jordan and Carlos)	Map

177

Group Planner

Plan for work on _____

Name					

Action Log

STEPS IN THE FORMATIVE ASSESSMENT PROCESS SUPPORTED BY THIS TOOL:

☑ Understand target	❑ Evaluate strengths and weaknesses
☑ Produce work	❑ Prescribe action for improvement
☑ Compare work with target	❑ Take action for improvement

HOW TO USE:

- Use this tool for individuals or small groups to keep track of progress on a long-term assignment or learning goal. The purpose is to help students monitor their own work.
- Have students list tasks in the first column. In the second and third columns, they should indicate the dates they worked on and completed each task.

WHAT TO LOOK FOR:

- Check that students are doing relevant tasks (tasks that will contribute to progress on the assignment and learning goals), and that the amount of time they are taking is realistic and appropriate for the tasks.
- Check that students are making appropriate progress so that they have time for all of the things they need to do to finish the assignment. For example, students who take most of their time in preliminary tasks will have to rush through the rest of the tasks to complete the assignment on time.

NEXT STEPS:

- Help students see the relationship between their work and their accomplishments.
- Help students see how listing the dates can keep them moving.

TIPS/VARIATIONS:

- Although this tool is designed as a log for recording work done, allow students to also use it as a planning tool, listing all the tasks they need to do at the beginning of the assignment and then keeping track of their progress by listing the dates.

Student Tools

Tools to Use During Individual or Group Work on Projects

Action Log

Assignment or learning goal   *Character Study: Compare and Contrast Lady Capulet and Lady Montague*

Steps	Dates worked on	Date completed
Read the play.	October 2–12	October 12
Identify and reread important scenes for Lady Capulet and Lady Montague.	October 12–13	October 13
Write first draft.	October 14–15	October 15
Edit, add some quotes, print.	October 16	October 16
Turn in final copy.		October 17

Action Log

Assignment or learning goal _____

_____

Steps	Dates worked on	Date completed

Student Tools

Evidence Basket

STEPS IN THE FORMATIVE ASSESSMENT PROCESS SUPPORTED BY THIS TOOL:

☑ Understand target   ☑ Evaluate strengths and weaknesses

❑ Produce work   ❑ Prescribe action for improvement

☑ Compare work with target   ❑ Take action for improvement

HOW TO USE:

- Use this tool to help students see the positive qualities in their own work—work that is completed but not graded yet. Students will need a copy of the assignment directions and rubric or grading criteria.
- Direct students to compare the quality of their own work with the criteria for the assignment. The "basket" metaphor helps them focus on the positive qualities of their work (what they did well). Use other tools if you want students to focus on areas for improvement (Conference Call, p. 189; Feedback Request Sheet, p. 193) or on both positives and negatives (Rubric's Cube, p. 196).

WHAT TO LOOK FOR:

- Check that student perceptions are accurate. Developing accurate self-evaluation skills will help students monitor their own learning.
- Check that students have identified all important aspects of the assignment. Some students, especially younger ones, will place more emphasis on surface characteristics (e.g., neatness) than on content.

NEXT STEPS:

- Keep the "basket" sheets from formative assessments (practice assignments). Then, at the time of summative assessment (graded assignment or test), have students reflect on the relationship between their practice and their accomplishments. The characteristics on the basketball (strengths during practice) should be related to the qualities reflected in their grades.

Student Tools

182 ❑

TIPS/VARIATIONS:

- Occasionally, there may be a time when all students did exceptionally well and an active celebration is called for. In such a case, students can complete the tools, crumple the sheets into paper balls, and each share one of their positive comments with the class as they try making a "basket" by shooting their paper ball into a wastebasket.

Evidence Basket

Assignment ___Speech about recycling___

How do you know your work is good?

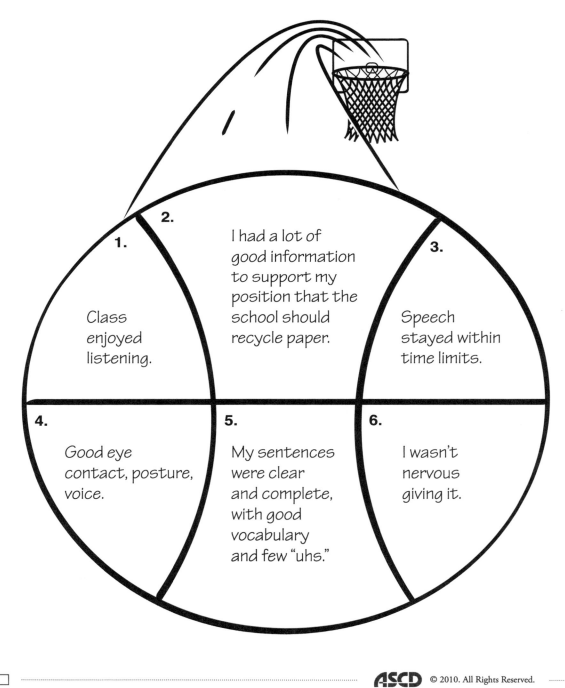

1. Class enjoyed listening.

2. I had a lot of good information to support my position that the school should recycle paper.

3. Speech stayed within time limits.

4. Good eye contact, posture, voice.

5. My sentences were clear and complete, with good vocabulary and few "uhs."

6. I wasn't nervous giving it.

Student Tools

Evidence Basket

Assignment _____

How do you know your work is good?

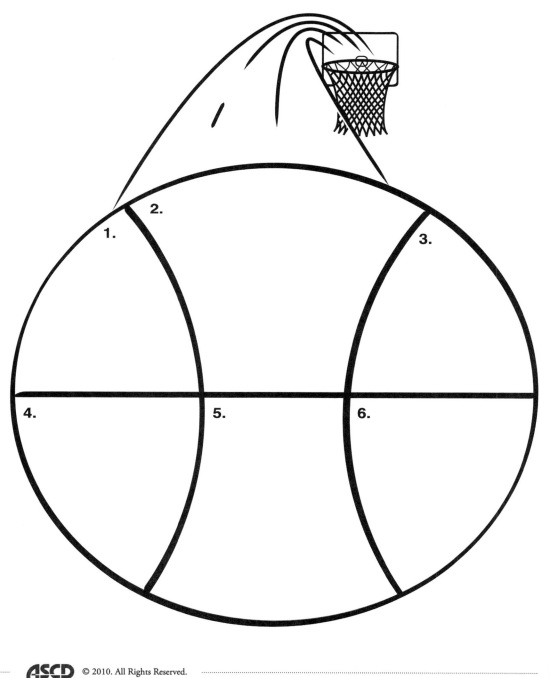

Under the Microscope

ACTION TOOL

STEPS IN THE FORMATIVE ASSESSMENT PROCESS SUPPORTED BY THIS TOOL:

☑ Understand target   ☑ Evaluate strengths and weaknesses
❑ Produce work   ❑ Prescribe action for improvement
☑ Compare work with target   ❑ Take action for improvement

HOW TO USE

- Identify a learning target and one assignment that you want students to analyze in detail. Remind students of the rubrics or other criteria for good work.
- Ask students to pretend they are putting their work under a microscope. Have them discuss briefly what microscopes do (enlarge images, make details visible, help us describe things). Point out that instead of enlarging their work, they will be looking it over slowly and in detail, as you have to do when you look at things under a microscope.
- Have students write what they "see" in their work when they do this detailed review.

WHAT TO LOOK FOR

- Look for accurate appraisal of the work against the criteria or performance standards.

NEXT STEPS

- If the work can be revised, have students use their notes as the basis for their revision.
- If revision is not appropriate for this work, ask students how they will apply what they learned from this exercise to their next similar assignment. Make sure a similar assignment is coming soon.

TIPS/VARIATIONS

- Students can do this in small groups or pairs, looking together at each other's work and agreeing on points before they write them.

Student Tools

Under the Microscope

Look at your work on *essay on the Declaration of Independence*

Put your work "under the microscope." Write a detailed description of what you see when you look over your work.

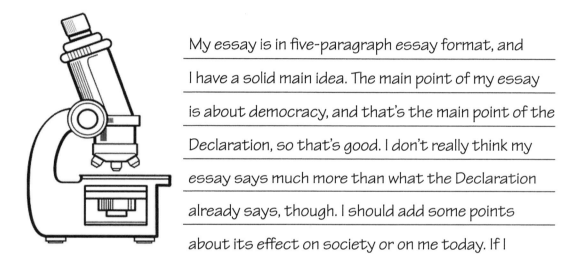

My essay is in five-paragraph essay format, and I have a solid main idea. The main point of my essay is about democracy, and that's the main point of the Declaration, so that's good. I don't really think my essay says much more than what the Declaration already says, though. I should add some points about its effect on society or on me today. If I do that, I'll have to reorganize the essay, and maybe spend less time on repeating stuff from the Declaration.

Under the Microscope

Look at your work on _____

Put your work "under the microscope." Write a detailed description of what you see when you look over your work.

_____

_____

_____

_____

_____

_____

_____

_____

_____

_____

_____

_____

_____

_____

_____

Conference Call

STEPS IN THE FORMATIVE ASSESSMENT PROCESS SUPPORTED BY THIS TOOL:

☑ Understand target   ☑ Evaluate strengths and weaknesses
❑ Produce work   ☑ Prescribe action for improvement
☑ Compare work with target   ❑ Take action for improvement

HOW TO USE:

- Use this tool when you are preparing for student-led student-teacher conferences about a learning objective or set of learning objectives (e.g., at the midpoint of a unit of instruction) or when you are preparing for a conference about a particular assignment.
- Ask students to list questions that they would like to talk with you about during the conference. Using these planned questions will help you use conference time efficiently. Having the students set the agenda will give them a feeling of ownership and will help ensure that you are giving them information they need and want to use.

WHAT TO LOOK FOR:

- Look for student questions that are clear and that ask for information students genuinely want or need to know to improve (as opposed to questions that amount to "fishing for compliments" or are so vague that the only answer is to repeat the assignment).
- Check that students did not miss something important about their work that needs to be discussed. If someone did miss something, ask that student to try to think of anything else you need to talk about together.

NEXT STEPS:

- Answer questions with clear suggestions about what students could do to improve.
- Observe student work after the conference to see what effect the students' questions and your discussion have on progress and learning.

Student Tools

TIPS/VARIATIONS:

- Use this tool both for the times you may plan to have a conference with each student in the class and for the times you plan conferences with just those students who have particular questions.
- Have students complete the sheets and leave them on a corner of their desk, so that you can do "desktop miniconferences" as you circulate through the room during seatwork time. Stop at desks where you see students have a question.

Conference Call

Look at your work on _solving equations in chapter 4_

Make a list of things you want to ask your teacher at a conference.

1. _How do I decide what to do to the equation first, if there are several_ _things that could be done?_

2. _Does it matter which side of the equation I try to get the "x" on?_

3. _Where can I find some extra practice problems?_

4. _____

5. _____

Conference Call

Look at your work on _____

Make a list of things you want to ask your teacher at a conference.

1. _____

_____

_____

2. _____

_____

_____

3. _____

_____

_____

4. _____

_____

_____

5. _____

_____

_____

Student Tools

Feedback Request Sheet

STEPS IN THE FORMATIVE ASSESSMENT PROCESS SUPPORTED BY THIS TOOL:

☑ Understand target   ☑ Evaluate strengths and weaknesses

☑ Produce work   ☑ Prescribe action for improvement

☑ Compare work with target   ☐ Take action for improvement

HOW TO USE:

- Use this tool when students are turning in a first draft of an assignment. You can use it with a final copy, if you wish, but students should understand that requests for feedback will not affect their grade for the assignment.
- Direct students to list aspects of the assignment on which they would like feedback.

WHAT TO LOOK FOR:

- Read each feedback request for the information it gives you about what the student thinks needs improvement or comment. Compare that with your own assessment.

NEXT STEPS:

- When you return the work with comments, provide just the feedback requested or the requested feedback plus any additional comments you wish to make. The purpose of having students ask for feedback is twofold: (1) to encourage self-evaluation and (2) to help you give students information they want to use.
- Answer the student's questions as clearly as you can. If appropriate, give the student a chance to act on your feedback on a new assignment or a revision of the old one.

TIPS/VARIATIONS:

- Let students use the tool as a cover sheet for the assignment and turn it in at the same time.
- After you return graded work (with feedback), have students use the tool to ask for clarification or expansion of the feedback you have given them. For example, you might have noted on an essay that a student should use more active verbs. The student might ask you to give an example or explain how to do that.

Student Tools

Feedback Request Sheet

Name _Keesha_

Date _May 3, 2010_

Assignment _Short story_

Please give feedback on these aspects of my work:

1. _The dialogue sounds dull. How do I make it sound more like real talk?_

2. _Is the story too short? It seems like a quick ending, but I couldn't think of any more to write._

3. _How was my proofreading?_

4. _____

Note: The more specific the requests are, the more detailed feedback can be.

Feedback Request Sheet

Name _____

Date _____

Assignment _____

Please give feedback on these aspects of my work:

1. _____

_____

_____

2. _____

_____

_____

3. _____

_____

_____

4. _____

_____

_____

Note: The more specific the requests are, the more detailed feedback can be.

Rubric's Cube

STEPS IN THE FORMATIVE ASSESSMENT PROCESS SUPPORTED BY THIS TOOL:

☑ Understand target
☐ Produce work
☑ Compare work with target

☑ Evaluate strengths and weaknesses
☑ Prescribe action for improvement
☑ Take action for improvement

HOW TO USE:

- Use this tool for student self-evaluation of a draft, of final work before turning it in, or of final work after it is returned. The tool is best used when students still have time to revise their work.
- Use this tool for peer evaluations.
- Write the items for your rubric on the left side of the cube, or instruct students to do so. Ask students to reflect on how their work fits into the descriptions of performance levels on the rubric. Instruct them to use the right side of the cube to respond to each item.

WHAT TO LOOK FOR:

- Check that student evaluations are accurate, relevant, and complete. Check that students' comments contain information they can use for improvement. If they do not, ask students why they wrote a comment or if they can think of anything else.

NEXT STEPS:

- Have students use their reflections to revise their work.
- If you wish, have students turn in these sheets with their revisions so that you can see what they intended and how successfully they met their own intentions.

TIPS/VARIATIONS:

- For analytic rubrics (several scales apply to one assignment), either use a separate cube for each scale or select one or two of the scales for self-evaluation.
- Adapt the cube for rubrics with more than four levels by adding another row or rows at the bottom.

Rubric's Cube

Assignment _Describe the main character in a story_

Use the cube to reflect on how your work does or does not match the rubric for the assignment.

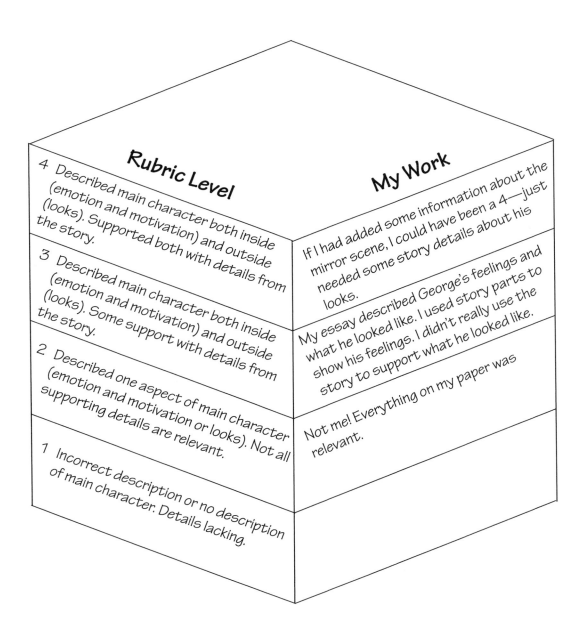

Rubric Level

4 Described main character both inside (emotion and motivation) and outside (looks). Supported both with details from the story.

3 Described main character both inside (emotion and motivation) and outside (looks). Some support with details from the story.

2 Described one aspect of main character (emotion and motivation or looks). Not all supporting details are relevant.

1 Incorrect description or no description of main character. Details lacking.

My Work

If I had added some information about the mirror scene, I could have been a 4—just needed some story details about his looks.

My essay described George's feelings and what he looked like. I used story parts to show his feelings. I didn't really use the story to support what he looked like.

Not me! Everything on my paper was relevant.

Rubric's Cube

Assignment _____

Use the cube to reflect on how your work does or does not match the rubric for the assignment.

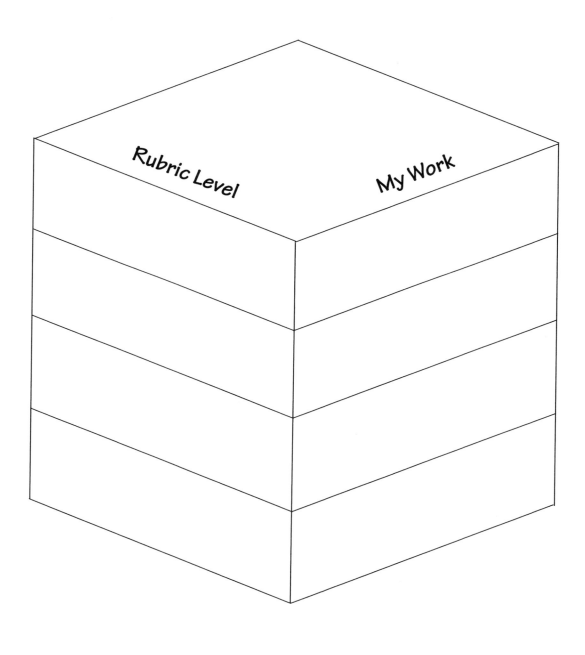

Student Tools

What Do You Think? What Do I Think?

STEPS IN THE FORMATIVE ASSESSMENT PROCESS SUPPORTED BY THIS TOOL:

☑ Understand target

☐ Produce work

☑ Compare work with target

☑ Evaluate strengths and weaknesses

☑ Prescribe action for improvement

☑ Take action for improvement

HOW TO USE:

- Select an assignment for which you will use peer evaluation. Have students share papers with their peers. Before beginning their evaluation, peers should review the directions for the assignment and the rubric or other evaluation criteria.
- Instruct the peer reviewers to write their comments on the left side ("What do you think?") of the tool and then fold the paper in half. Direct the reviewers to evaluate the work by stating what's good about it and giving suggestions for improvement.
- Direct students to do a self-evaluation of their work on the right side of the paper, without looking at the peer comments. Then, let them open the paper, compare the comments, and plan revisions accordingly.

WHAT TO LOOK FOR:

- Check that comments are accurate and relevant, and that they contain suggestions for improvement or information about what was good. Check that peer comments are respectful. If necessary, teach students how to make comments appropriately (e.g., demonstrate that comments like "This is bad" don't help the student, but comments like "I can't tell which character you agree with" are helpful).

NEXT STEPS:

- Decide whether the peer and self-evaluations are sufficient for students to make effective revisions. For some assignments, you may wish to look over the suggestions yourself and make additional comments, taking advantage of the information in students' evaluations.

Student Tools

 199

- Have students use the evaluations to revise their work. Remind them they should decide how to use the information. For example, they don't have to make a change recommended by a peer if they don't think it's a good suggestion.

TIPS/VARIATIONS:

- Let students use their review sheets to evaluate their revisions before turning them in.
- Have students turn in their review sheets with their revised assignment, so that you can see where and why the changes were made.

What Do You Think? What Do I Think?

Assignment ___Short story___

First, ask a classmate to comment on your work; then, fold the paper in half. Next, write your own comments without looking at the notes your classmate wrote. Finally, unfold the paper and use both sets of comments to revise your work.

What Do You Think?	What Do I Think?
I liked it! The scary monkey was really scary. At the beginning, the doctor in the lab reminded me a lot of the Frankenstein story. Is there a way you could make it more original? At the end, if you want us to wonder whether the monkey got away, there needs to be some reason for it.	This was fun to write. I got some ideas from a couple movies, so I hope it's not too obvious. I think the ending is too abrupt. I just say, "They killed the monkey. Or did they?" It was supposed to sound sinister, but it just sounds dumb. I should say why they could be wrong.

What Do You Think? What Do I Think?

Assignment _____

First, ask a classmate to comment on your work; then, fold the paper in half. Next, write your own comments without looking at the notes your classmate wrote. Finally, unfold the paper and use both sets of comments to revise your work.

What Do You Think?	What Do I Think?

Peer Review Form

ACTION TOOL

STEPS IN THE FORMATIVE ASSESSMENT PROCESS SUPPORTED BY THIS TOOL:

☑ Understand target   ☑ Evaluate strengths and weaknesses

☐ Produce work   ☑ Prescribe action for improvement

☑ Compare work with target   ☑ Take action for improvement

HOW TO USE:

- Select an assignment for which you will use peer evaluation. Have students share papers with their peers. Before beginning their evaluation, peers should review the directions for the assignment and the rubric or other evaluation criteria.
- Direct peer reviewers to write comments about the assignment's strengths and weaknesses and share them with the authors.

WHAT TO LOOK FOR:

- Check that comments are accurate and relevant, and that they contain suggestions for improvement or information about what was good. Check that peer comments are respectful. If necessary, teach students how to make comments appropriately (e.g., demonstrate that comments like "This is bad" don't help the student, but comments like "I can't tell which character you agree with" are helpful).

NEXT STEPS:

- Students can use the comments for revisions and for future work.
- Decide whether the peer evaluations are sufficient for revisions. For some assignments, you may also wish to look over the suggestions yourself and make additional comments, taking advantage of the information in students' evaluations.

TIPS/VARIATIONS:

- Let students use their peer review sheets to evaluate their revisions before turning them in.
- Have students turn in their peer review sheets with their revised assignment, so that you can see where and why the changes were made.

    ☐ 203

Student Tools

EXAMPLE

Peer Review Form

Assignment _Short story "Scary Monkey"_

Use the directions and the rubric for the assignment as guidelines. Write the strengths and weaknesses of your classmate's work. Make positive suggestions.

Work by _Robin_   Review by _Lawinda_

Strengths	Weaknesses
Easy to read, good English, nice handwriting.	Bert the doctor was too much like the Frankenstein story. Be more original?
Three separate scenes—lab, house, and park—have clear transitions.	If you want to suggest the monkey got away at the end, give a reason to think so.
Nice development. In each scene the monkey gets a little "badder."	

Peer Review Form

Assignment _____

Use the directions and the rubric for the assignment as guidelines. Write the strengths and weaknesses of your classmate's work. Make positive suggestions.

Work by _____   Review by _____

Strengths	Weaknesses

ACTION TOOL Groupies

STEPS IN THE FORMATIVE ASSESSMENT PROCESS SUPPORTED BY THIS TOOL:

☑ Understand target   ☑ Evaluate strengths and weaknesses
☐ Produce work   ☑ Prescribe action for improvement
☑ Compare work with target   ☐ Take action for improvement

HOW TO USE:

- Use this tool when students are working in small, collaborative work groups.
- Put group members' names in the "Name" column.
- Instruct students to work together to put comments in the boxes, with one person acting as the scribe. This helps them talk together about what they want from each other as participants in the group. It does not work well to have them "rate" each other individually, on separate sheets, because they would feel like they were "grading" each other, which would lead to judgmental instead of substantive comments.
- Use this tool for group communication, feedback, and improvement. Establish an environment in which it is safe to "need improvement" or students will not be able to give each other honest feedback.

WHAT TO LOOK FOR:

- Check that comments are accurate, relevant, and respectful.

NEXT STEPS:

- Observe the group's behavior to see that the discussion about the group process is helping them work together better. Intervene if students are not able to resolve an issue after working on it themselves.

TIPS/VARIATIONS:

- Make this kind of group reflection a regular part of group work, perhaps during the last 5 or 10 minutes of work sessions periodically.

Student Tools

206 ☐

ASCD

Tools to Use During Individual or Group Work on Projects

- If necessary, teach students how to avoid making judgmental remarks (e.g., "That's bad") but to ask instead for something specific (e.g., "We need you to write the summary").
- Use this tool to encourage communication among students. Do not let it become a way for students to "tell on" each other to you.

Student Tools

Groupies

`EXAMPLE`

Group Name *Group I, George Washington Report*   Date *9/25/09*

Rules for giving group feedback:

- **Respect** group members.
- **Tell why** each good contribution was helpful.
- **Ask** a group member for something if needed.

Name	Comments about how he or she		
	Prepared	**Listened**	**Contributed**
Bill B.			Brought a picture of George Washington. Asked a good question about the next meeting.
Sally M.	Read the whole chapter next time.		Good idea to assign everyone to write paragraphs for next time.
Anson R.		Please listen to everyone.	Wrote the introduction for the report. Volunteered to be the narrator.
Lywinda T.			Wrote the section about George Washington as a general.

Groupies

Group Name _____   Date _____

Rules for giving group feedback:
- **Respect** group members.
- **Tell why** each good contribution was helpful.
- **Ask** a group member for something if needed.

Name	Comments about how he or she		
	Prepared	**Listened**	**Contributed**

Student Tools

Mission: Possible

STEPS IN THE FORMATIVE ASSESSMENT PROCESS SUPPORTED BY THIS TOOL:

☑ Understand target   ❑ Evaluate strengths and weaknesses

☑ Produce work   ❑ Prescribe action for improvement

❑ Compare work with target   ❑ Take action for improvement

HOW TO USE:

- Select an assignment in which you want students to use strategies for both how to do the work and how to enjoy it—that is, to monitor and manage their motivation. The purpose is to point out that much of motivation can be under students' own control.

- Ask students to reflect on several different ways they could approach the assignment and decide which ones are more and less motivating—that is, "boring" and "interesting" in student language.

WHAT TO LOOK FOR:

- Check that students' strategies are realistic and relevant. Accept students' reported feelings of "boring" or "interesting." You may want to ask why students think various approaches will be boring or interesting.

- Use what you learn about student interest to help in planning this and future assignments.

NEXT STEPS:

- Try to help students understand that a few "boring" steps may be required in otherwise "interesting" work in order to complete the assignment. All work, however, can and should have at least some interesting aspects. Students may need practice to find them and to get into the habit of looking for them.

TIPS/VARIATIONS:

- Allow students to work in pairs on this assignment and discuss their approaches to the work as they note them.

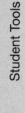

Student Tools

Mission: Possible

Assignment _Civil War notebook/report_

Ways to do this that are

Boring	Interesting
Work in the library by myself. Get all the sources and then read them all at once. Write the report by hand.	Use the Internet at Ryan's house. Add pictures. Share notes with Cole. Read a bit at a time. Write the report on a computer.

Mission: Possible

Assignment _____

Ways to do this that are

Boring	Interesting

Student Tools

Minute Math

STEPS IN THE FORMATIVE ASSESSMENT PROCESS SUPPORTED BY THIS TOOL:

☑ Understand target   ❑ Evaluate strengths and weaknesses

☑ Produce work   ❑ Prescribe action for improvement

☑ Compare work with target   ❑ Take action for improvement

HOW TO USE:

- Use this tool with repeated tests, such as weekly timed tests of math facts.
- Ask students to predict their score (in percentage) and color in the bar graph to represent it.
- After the test, have students graph their actual score. Students will be able to see their "steps" of progress, and their predictions should generally become more accurate over time.

WHAT TO LOOK FOR:

- Look for fairly accurate predictions. Look for gradual improvement over time.
- If some students overpredict or underpredict at first, check that they become more accurate with later tests.

NEXT STEPS:

- Have students reflect on their progress and plan the strategies they will use to improve each time. Students should come to see that studying and improving are under their control.

TIPS/VARIATIONS:

- For timed tests, students who reach 100 before the rest of the class may choose to try to better their time in subsequent weeks.

Source: From Patricia Pozza, Deer Lakes School District, Russellton, Pennsylvania. Used by permission.

Student Tools

Minute Math

Name Sally

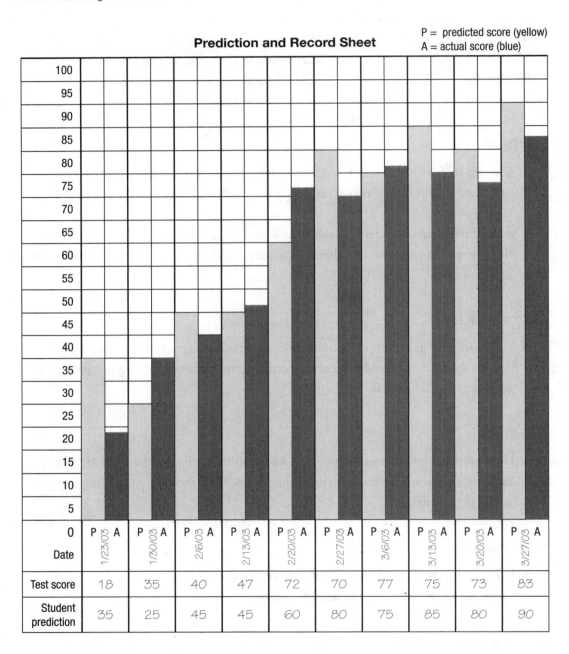

Prediction and Record Sheet

P = predicted score (yellow)
A = actual score (blue)

	P 1/23/03 A	P 1/30/03 A	P 2/6/03 A	P 2/13/03 A	P 2/20/03 A	P 2/27/03 A	P 3/6/03 A	P 3/13/03 A	P 3/20/03 A	P 3/27/03 A
Date	1/23/03	1/30/03	2/6/03	2/13/03	2/20/03	2/27/03	3/6/03	3/13/03	3/20/03	3/27/03
Test score	18	35	40	47	72	70	77	75	73	83
Student prediction	35	25	45	45	60	80	75	85	80	90

Minute Math

Name _____

Prediction and Record Sheet

P = predicted score (yellow)
A = actual score (blue)

	P	A	P	A	P	A	P	A	P	A	P	A	P	A	P	A	P	A	P	A
100																				
95																				
90																				
85																				
80																				
75																				
70																				
65																				
60																				
55																				
50																				
45																				
40																				
35																				
30																				
25																				
20																				
15																				
10																				
5																				
0	P	A	P	A	P	A	P	A	P	A	P	A	P	A	P	A	P	A	P	A
Date																				
Test score																				
Student prediction																				

Awesome and On My Way

ACTION TOOL

STEPS IN THE FORMATIVE ASSESSMENT PROCESS SUPPORTED BY THIS TOOL:

☑ Understand target
☐ Produce work
☑ Compare work with target

☑ Evaluate strengths and weaknesses
☑ Prescribe action for improvement
☑ Take action for improvement

HOW TO USE:

- Use this tool as part of preparation for a test. Students should be able to differentiate the content they need to review lightly from the content they need to learn more deeply.
- Have students prepare their lists in plenty of time to use them in studying for a test or exam.

WHAT TO LOOK FOR:

- Look for an accurate appraisal of which topics are in which category.
- Look to see that students are using the results of their categorizing to allot their study time and energy accordingly.

NEXT STEPS:

- After the test, ask students to reflect on the benefits of organizing their study time in this way. What was effective? Were they good judges of how much studying the various topics required?

TIPS/VARIATIONS:

- Students can use this tool to study together. In small groups, students who have topics in the "awesome" category can quiz those who are "on my way" on that topic. If all students are "on my way," they can help each other reread material from the text, practice with problems or vocabulary words, and so on.

Awesome and On My Way

EXAMPLE

Think about the material you will study for the ___English Colonies 1607–1750___ test.
Divide it into two categories.

I am
Awesome

**I know this material well
and will briefly review it:**

Colonial governments

- 3 kinds
  - royal
  - proprietary
  - self-governing
- governors & legislatures

Life in English colonies

- religion
- work
- climate
- location

I am
On My Way

**I will concentrate
on this material:**

Trade & commerce

- mercantile theory of trade
- British navigation and trade acts
- triangular trade, including slave trade
- "salutary neglect"

Relations with Native Americans

- influences of politics, resources, and the French

Awesome and On My Way

Think about the material you will study for the _____ test.
Divide it into two categories.

I am

Awesome

**I know this material well
and will briefly review it:**

I am

On My Way

**I will concentrate
on this material:**

Cell Phone

STEPS IN THE FORMATIVE ASSESSMENT PROCESS SUPPORTED BY THIS TOOL:

☑ Understand target   ☑ Evaluate strengths and weaknesses
❑ Produce work   ☑ Prescribe action for improvement
❑ Compare work with target ☑ Take action for improvement

HOW TO USE:

- Use this tool as part of preparation for a test. Students should be able to describe the content they need to review and the methods they will use to do that.
- Suggest that students study together. Helping a friend is a positive way to approach giving study advice, and what's good for the friend should be good for the student, too.

WHAT TO LOOK FOR:

- Check that the students' descriptions of the content to study are accurate and complete. If not, remind them of what will be on the test.
- Check that the methods students suggest will be effective and productive. Different students will suggest different methods. Many may be able to say why they think their study methods work. Finding out about your students' study methods should give you insights into their thinking.

NEXT STEPS:

- Have students check their test performance against their planning. Were their methods effective? What might they do differently next time? Students should come to see that their achievement is related to their effort.

TIPS/VARIATIONS:

- Encourage students to actually call a friend and arrange to study together, as appropriate.

Student Tools

Cell Phone

Pretend you are going to call a friend tonight about the ___Introduction to Functions___
test. What advice would you give your friend about what and how to study?

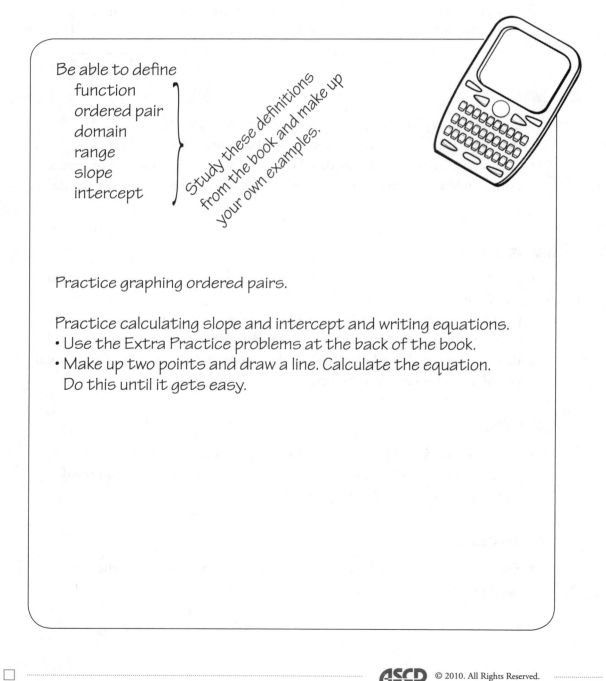

Be able to define
    function
    ordered pair
    domain
    range
    slope
    intercept

Study these definitions from the book and make up your own examples.

Practice graphing ordered pairs.

Practice calculating slope and intercept and writing equations.
• Use the Extra Practice problems at the back of the book.
• Make up two points and draw a line. Calculate the equation.
  Do this until it gets easy.

Cell Phone

Pretend you are going to call a friend tonight about the _____
test. What advice would you give your friend about what and how to study?

Home Help Sheet

STEPS IN THE FORMATIVE ASSESSMENT PROCESS SUPPORTED BY THIS TOOL:

- ☑ Understand target
- ☑ Produce work
- ☑ Compare work with target
- ☑ Evaluate strengths and weaknesses
- ☑ Prescribe action for improvement
- ☑ Take action for improvement

HOW TO USE:

- Use this tool for students who need to keep track of their studying, although it is also helpful for any student who wants an organizing tool for studying at home.
- Direct students to record what and how they studied, according to the column headings on the chart.

WHAT TO LOOK FOR:

- Check that students studied relevant material and used appropriate methods.
- Check that studying is regular and of appropriate duration. Remind students that daily small study periods are usually more productive than large cramming sessions.

NEXT STEPS:

- Encourage students to evaluate how well a study plan worked for a test and then to adjust their study patterns accordingly in the future.
- Make explicit connections between study and achievement. Help students see that the effort they expend is related to what they learn. When students can make connections between effort and achievement, they are more likely to develop internal motivation.

TIPS/VARIATIONS:

- Encourage students to organize and plan all their studying, not just those occasions where you use a tool like this one. Students who are self-regulated learners develop skills for lifelong learning.

Student Tools

Home Help Sheet

Test _Parts of Speech_

Scheduled for _Tuesday, May 16_

Day	What I Studied	How Long I Studied	Alone or with Help?
Monday 5/8	nouns	15 min.	alone
Tuesday 5/9	nouns, verbs	20 min.	alone
Wednesday 5/10	adjectives, adverbs	20 min.	alone
Thursday 5/11	adverbs	15 min.	Mom helped me with the practice exercises.
Saturday 5/13	nouns, verbs, adjectives, adverbs	1/2 hr.	I did the practice test alone and Mom went over it with me.
Monday 5/15	nouns, verbs, adjectives, adverbs	1/2 hr.	alone

Home Help Sheet

Test _____

Scheduled for _____

Day	What I Studied	How Long I Studied	Alone or with Help?

Student Tools

T.E.S.T.

STEPS IN THE FORMATIVE ASSESSMENT PROCESS SUPPORTED BY THIS TOOL:

☑ Understand target	☑ Evaluate strengths and weaknesses
☐ Produce work	☑ Prescribe action for improvement
☑ Compare work with target	☑ Take action for improvement

HOW TO USE:

- Use this tool as part of preparation for a test. Students should be able to plan their studying **T**ime, **E**ffort, **S**ubjects (topics or material), and **T**actics (study strategies).
- Have students do their analyses in plenty of time to use them in studying for a test or exam.

WHAT TO LOOK FOR:

- Look for students' accurate appraisal of their own study needs.
- Look to see that students are using the results of their analyses to allot their study time and energy accordingly.

NEXT STEPS:

- After the test, ask students to reflect on the benefits of organizing their study time in this way. What was effective? Were they good judges of their study needs?

TIPS/VARIATIONS:

- Have students get in the habit of doing the "T.E.S.T." analysis for every test they must study for, in your class and others, as a regular part of their test preparation.

T.E.S.T.

Use this chart to plan your studying for the ___quadratic equations___ test.

Time — When and how long will I study?

Test is Friday 4th period.
Study: ½ hr. Wed. night, 1 hr. Thurs. night.
Review in homeroom Fri. morning

Effort — How hard do I need to work to prepare for this test?

Medium. I am better at solving than graphing, so I should spend more time on graphing.

Subjects — What topics or materials will this test cover?

Solving quadratic equations with 1 variable.
Graphing quadratic equations of the form $y = ax^2 + bx + c$
Transforming quadratic equations that aren't in that form so they can be graphed.

Tactics — What study strategies will I use?

Use sample problems from text supplement and
Mr. Clayton's review sheets.
Do extra problems in graphing.

T.E.S.T.

Use this chart to plan your studying for the _____ test.

Time   **When and how long will I study?**

Effort   **How hard do I need to work to prepare for this test?**

Subjects   **What topics or materials will this test cover?**

Tactics   **What study strategies will I use?**

Student Tools

ACTION TOOL "I Get It"

STEPS IN THE FORMATIVE ASSESSMENT PROCESS SUPPORTED BY THIS TOOL:

☑ Understand target   ☑ Evaluate strengths and weaknesses
☐ Produce work   ☑ Prescribe action for improvement
☑ Compare work with target   ☐ Take action for improvement

HOW TO USE:

- Use this tool with learning targets or assignments in which students need to study concepts.
- Ask students to reflect on what they do and don't understand, and then to write their thoughts in the appropriate boxes.
- Have students use their lists to help with studying for tests, peer tutoring, and review and practice activities.

WHAT TO LOOK FOR:

- Check that students' reflections accurately reflect their understanding.
- Help students use the evidence from their work in their reflections (e.g., questions missed on exercises, reading assignments they didn't understand, and so on, for the "I don't get it" box; questions answered and assignments understood for the "I get it" box).

NEXT STEPS:

- Celebrate the "light bulb" or "I get it" side of the tool by affirming comments and by asking students to help others with those concepts.
- Encourage students to work on the "question mark" or "I don't get it" side with study and practice until they do understand.

TIPS/VARIATIONS:

- Whenever possible, help students make connections between their effort (for example, these reflections and the resulting actions) and their achievement. Students who see learning as under their control will be better learners.

"I Get It"

Learning target or assignment <u>Photosynthesis—understanding how plans make food</u>

I don't get these things.	**I get it! I understand these things.**
how the light-dependent and light-independent processes are related I get mixed up about the way the chemicals and energy work in the chemical reactions in the 2 processes.	the chemical formula water + CO_2 –> sugar & oxygen the parts of the plant how chlorophyll and other pigments capture the light as energy for the process the structure of a chloroplast

Student Tools

"I Get It"

Learning target or assignment _____

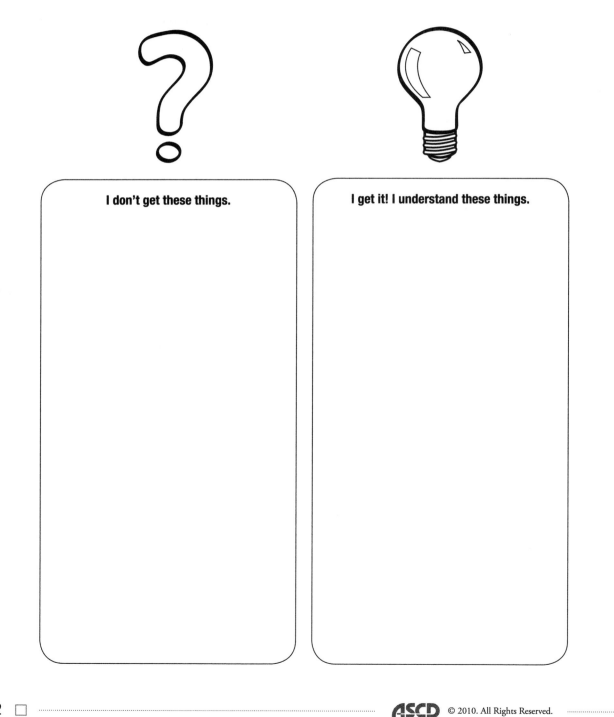

I don't get these things.	I get it! I understand these things.

Tools to Use •••
After Summative Assessment

Do-Overs

STEPS IN THE FORMATIVE ASSESSMENT PROCESS SUPPORTED BY THIS TOOL:

☑ Understand target   ☑ Evaluate strengths and weaknesses

☐ Produce work   ☑ Prescribe action for improvement

☑ Compare work with target   ☑ Take action for improvement

HOW TO USE:

- Use this tool after a test, an assignment, or a project is completed and graded. Give students an opportunity to reflect on what they would have done differently.
- Use the opportunity to teach students how to reflect on what they would have done differently in study, preparation, or other work related to the assignment. "I would get them all right" is not a helpful comment. "I would have studied further ahead" and "I would have found some more information about cell structure" are helpful kinds of comments.

WHAT TO LOOK FOR:

- Check that the strategies the student suggests are realistic and are related to the performance in question.
- Use the opportunity to point out to students the connections between effort, engagement with materials and content, and achievement. Students who see a connection between the focus and intensity of their work and achievement are more likely to develop internal motivation to learn.

NEXT STEPS:

- In brief individual conferences, review each student's comments. If both you and the student agree that it is reasonable to do so, give the student a chance to do the assignment over. If a student asks on his or her own to redo an assignment, encourage the student to use the reflections to justify the request. It is not fair to ask students to contemplate revisions or redoing if such options are impractical or unreasonable. Strategies that are likely to lead to improvement are worth a second chance.

Student Tools

TIPS/VARIATIONS:

- If you give students an opportunity to redo an assignment, make sure that you have a grading policy to go along with it. Students will want to know about their grades. The policy needs to be fair to all students, realistic, and manageable. The grade needs to ultimately reflect the student's true level of achievement, not level of effort.

Student Tools

Do-Overs

EXAMPLE

Assignment Report on Tundra

Grade B-

Reflect on the test or assignment listed above.

If you had it to do over again, what would you do differently?

I would have used a map to show locations of tundras around the world.

I would have more information about the animals and vegetation.(I wrote mostly about weather.)

I would look for some pictures to go with the sections of the report.

Would you like a chance to do it over?

Yes

Do-Overs

Assignment _____

Grade _____

Reflect on the test or assignment listed above.

If you had it to do over again, what would you do differently?

Would you like a chance to do it over?

Student Tools

Dear Diary

STEPS IN THE FORMATIVE ASSESSMENT PROCESS SUPPORTED BY THIS TOOL:

☑ Understand target   ☑ Evaluate strengths and weaknesses

☐ Produce work   ☑ Prescribe action for improvement

☑ Compare work with target   ☐ Take action for improvement

HOW TO USE:

- Use this journaling tool for formative assessment on a regular basis, referring to both assignments and work habits. Specific journal entries can also be used for reflection about particular learning targets.

- Initiate student self-reflection with a focus question. The question can be general—for example, a reflection each week on "How did I do my work this week?" or "What did I learn in math class this week?" Questions can also be focused on particular learning targets—for example, "How much did I improve in long division this week?"

- Let students know ahead of time whether you are going to look at their journals. Because formative assessment involves teachers and students communicating about how students are doing in reference to learning targets, we recommend that you tell students you will look at their journals. Even though you will see only what the student decides to share with you, both you and the student will be able to act on the information.

WHAT TO LOOK FOR:

- Look for comments that are realistic and that explicitly or implicitly contain direction for further work and improvement. You may need to teach students how to write these kinds of comments and then provide time for students to practice writing them.

NEXT STEPS:

- Where appropriate, help students use their reflections in their future work. If you see comments or patterns of comments that give you ideas to suggest to a student, use them.

     ☐ 239

Student Tools

TIPS/VARIATIONS:

- Use this tool as a stand-alone activity or as part of a regular self-evaluation journal.
- Suggest that students use extra notebook paper if they need more space.

Dear Diary

EXAMPLE

Focus Question _How did I do in English class this week (first 2 acts of <u>Romeo and Juliet</u>)?_

○ **Dear Diary,**

I like the story of Romeo and Juliet, so I started out with enthusiasm. Monday and Tuesday I read the whole assignment each night. But I found the reading hard, and it was easier to listen in class than to read it all myself.

○

Mrs. Smith gave us a summary of each act, and that helped. I should try rereading Acts 1 and 2 with the summary beside me. I need to do that before we start on Acts 3 and 4 next week so I know what's going on.

○

   ☐ 241

Student Tools

Dear Diary

Focus Question _____

○ **Dear Diary,**

○

○

Progress Map

STEPS IN THE FORMATIVE ASSESSMENT PROCESS SUPPORTED BY THIS TOOL:

☑ Understand target   ☑ Evaluate strengths and weaknesses

❑ Produce work   ☑ Prescribe action for improvement

☑ Compare work with target   ☑ Take action for improvement

HOW TO USE:

- Use this tool to help students keep track of their work in a content area. Encourage students to use the chart as a real "map" of where they are going (not just a list of grades) by using the "Notes" section to comment on what they learned and what they want to work on.
- Use this tool only if your sequence of assignments forms a recognizable body of work. This will be the case in most content areas if you are following a clear curriculum and standards document. If the collection of work is a series of unrelated assignments, it won't "add up" to anything for the student.

WHAT TO LOOK FOR:

- Check for progress in achievement. Review the "Notes" section to check for students' deepening understanding of what they are learning.

NEXT STEPS:

- Use the information to help you understand the students' perceptions of their own progress. This should help you in instruction, in conversations about student work, and in designing questions for students.
- Help students avoid wanting just linear "progress," in which each grade is higher than the previous one. Assignments differ in their level of challenge and in the learning targets they embody. Help the students see their progress in learning, not numbers.

TIPS/VARIATIONS:

- Use this tool again, after several weeks, because students may benefit from reflecting on their progress and on what they learned as a whole.

      ☐ 243

Student Tools

EXAMPLE

Progress Map

Content Area __Romeo and Juliet__

Graded Work	Quiz on Acts 1–2	Quiz on Acts 3–4	Quiz on Act 5	Newspaper story: "Montague-Capulet Feud"	Character study: Lady C & Lady M	Paper: Elizabethan Weddings	Act 2, Scene 2 group pre-sentation	Romeo and Juliet test
Date Returned	Oct. 2	Oct. 9	Oct. 16	Oct. 17	Oct. 18	Oct. 19	Oct. 20	Oct. 23
Grade	79	82	95	100	89	95	A	92
Notes	The language is hard. I need to read each act a couple times.	Still hard. I have to "trans-late" the English!	Getting it!	This was easier because I used "regu-lar" English.	Still having trouble getting the shades of meaning from the Shake-spearean language.	This was fun. I can write well if I can use informa-tion I under-stand.	We worked hard at this. I did some great costume and prop work. I'm glad I didn't have to say many lines.	

Tools to Use After Summative Assessment

Progress Map

Content Area _____

Graded Work	Date Returned	Grade	Notes

Student Tools

Strengths and Weaknesses

STEPS IN THE FORMATIVE ASSESSMENT PROCESS SUPPORTED BY THIS TOOL:

☑ Understand target
❑ Produce work
☑ Compare work with target

☑ Evaluate strengths and weaknesses
❑ Prescribe action for improvement
❑ Take action for improvement

HOW TO USE:

- Use this tool to help individuals, small groups, or large groups evaluate their work on an assignment.
- Remind students to refer not only to the work itself but also to the directions and rubric as they use this tool.
- If a group evaluation is used, require students to give reasons for classifying an aspect of the work as a strength or a weakness.

WHAT TO LOOK FOR:

- Check that the comments about strengths and weaknesses are relevant, accurate, and complete.

NEXT STEPS:

- If comments are relevant, accurate, and complete, you and the students can use the feedback for improvement in future work.
- If comments are not accurate, ask students to explain their reasoning and evidence. If comments are not relevant, refer students to the directions or the rubric for the assignment. If comments are not complete, ask students if they can think of anything else.

TIPS/VARIATIONS:

- Have students use this tool individually for self-evaluation and then share it in small groups for additional peer comments.
- Remind students to criticize or praise the work, not the person, and to be respectful. You may need to make this an explicit rule.

Student Tools

Strengths and Weaknesses

Assignment _Still-life painting_

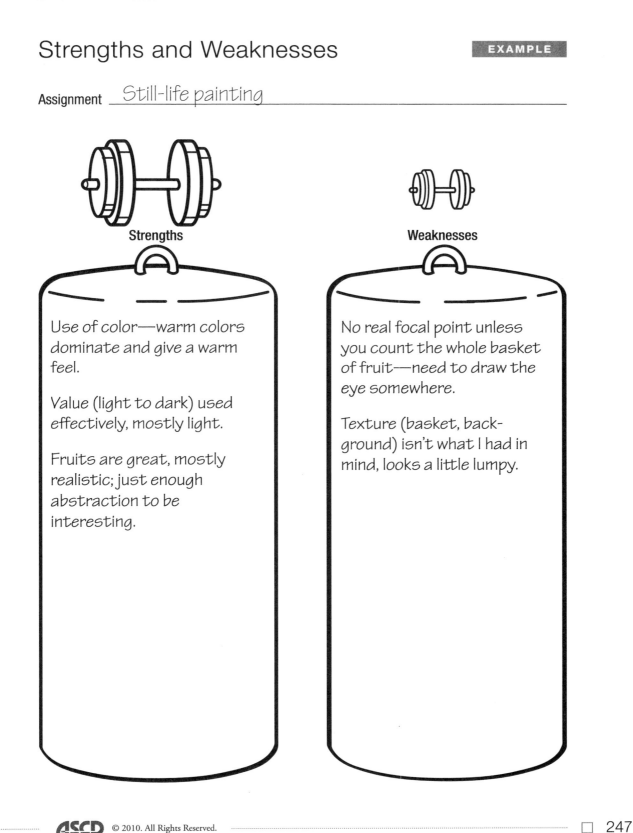

Strengths

Use of color—warm colors dominate and give a warm feel.

Value (light to dark) used effectively, mostly light.

Fruits are great, mostly realistic; just enough abstraction to be interesting.

Weaknesses

No real focal point unless you count the whole basket of fruit—need to draw the eye somewhere.

Texture (basket, background) isn't what I had in mind, looks a little lumpy.

Student Tools

Strengths and Weaknesses

Assignment _____

Exercise Program

STEPS IN THE FORMATIVE ASSESSMENT PROCESS SUPPORTED BY THIS TOOL:

☑ Understand target	☐ Evaluate strengths and weaknesses
☐ Produce work	☑ Prescribe action for improvement
☐ Compare work with target	☑ Take action for improvement

HOW TO USE:

- Use this tool in conjunction with the Strengths and Weaknesses tool (p. 246), if desired.
- Help students select an area that needs improvement and list one or two skills in that area to practice.
- Have students identify one or two exercises to strengthen each identified skill and prescribe how long and how often to practice. If appropriate, talk about how a coach might prescribe a set of exercises for an athlete or how a physical therapist might prescribe a set of exercises for a patient.

WHAT TO LOOK FOR:

- Check that the targeted area and skills are important and worth the practice time.
- Check that the exercises identified are a good match to the skill and to the student's level, that the time estimates are realistic and feasible, and that any materials needed (e.g., flash cards) are available.

NEXT STEPS:

- Ask students to follow their prescribed exercise program for an agreed-upon amount of time (e.g., a week) and then reevaluate.

TIPS/VARIATIONS:

- Use this tool in conjunction with other classroom instructional routines, such as learning centers, supply corners, seatwork time, and so on. For example, instead of a group doing a prescribed seat assignment while you are working with another group, give students time to work on their own prescriptions.
- Use this tool in conjunction with homework assignments.

Student Tools

Exercise Program

Practice area ___Composition in drawing and painting___

EXAMPLE

Target Skill	Exercise	How Long	How Often	Exercise	How Long	How Often
Create a focal point	Study the masters—pick paintings from book and describe the focal point of each.	10 min.	2 times a week	Freehand sketch—concentrate on focal point.	10 min.	2 times a week
Texture	"Doodle time" on plain paper—practice making textured shapes.	10 min.	Once a day			

Exercise Program

Practice area _____

Target Skill	Exercise	How Long	How Often	Exercise	How Long	How Often

Goal Setting

STEPS IN THE FORMATIVE ASSESSMENT PROCESS SUPPORTED BY THIS TOOL:

☑ Understand target	☐ Evaluate strengths and weaknesses
☐ Produce work	☑ Prescribe action for improvement
☐ Compare work with target	☑ Take action for improvement

HOW TO USE:

- Use this tool to help students set learning goals. The purpose is to help students see that they can control their learning. Students should develop skills in monitoring and adjusting their own goals. Working toward goals they have set themselves is more purposeful and meaningful (and usually, therefore, more motivating) than passively accepting teacher-imposed goals for their learning.
- Ask students to think of up to three goals in an area of study that they would like to work on. They should not "pull these out of a hat," but should think about their work. Goal setting is a next step after self-assessment.

WHAT TO LOOK FOR:

- Check that the students' goals are realistic and achievable. Check that they fit with the curriculum and instruction.
- Allow different students to identify different goals for special attention.

NEXT STEPS:

- Help students find strategies to work on the goals they have selected.
- Have students monitor their progress toward their goals.
- As goals are accomplished, help students celebrate their achievements and select other goals.

TIPS/VARIATIONS:

- Use the tool in conjunction with specific lessons or units for the whole class, or use for selected students as part of differentiated instruction.

Goal Setting

Topic or skill area ___proofs in geometry___

Set three goals to work for.

1.

Draw and label diagrams better.

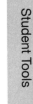

GOAL

How will you work on them?

2.

Memorize the axioms and learn the theorems.

Complete all homework.

Find a study partner.

Take my math book home at night.

3.

Try to think more logically.

Goal Setting

Topic or skill area _____

Set three goals to work for.

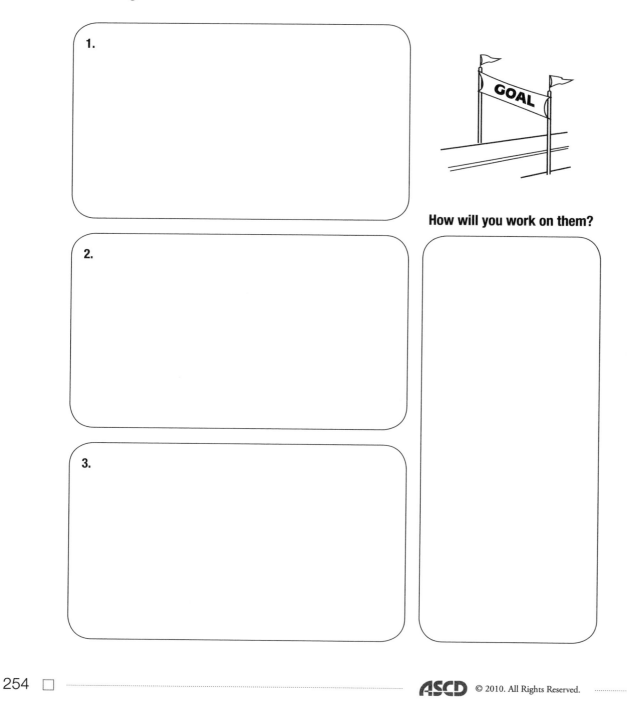

1.

GOAL

How will you work on them?

2.

3.

Student Tools

Effort-o-Meter

ACTION TOOL

STEPS IN THE FORMATIVE ASSESSMENT PROCESS SUPPORTED BY THIS TOOL:

☑ Understand target
☐ Produce work
☑ Compare work with target

☑ Evaluate strengths and weaknesses
☑ Prescribe action for improvement
☐ Take action for improvement

HOW TO USE:

- Use this tool after a test, project, or report has been completed and turned in, but not returned to students yet. The idea is to get students to gauge their effort without being influenced once they see the grade they received.
- Ask students to identify how hard they concentrated (investment of mental effort), how much time they spent, and how carefully they worked. It is important to separate these. Some research suggests that if simply asked, "How hard did you work?" students will respond in terms of the amount of time an assignment took. The point of this tool is to encourage students to think about several ways of expending effort.
- For younger students, give oral directions about how to color in the meters. Use the template on which the meters take up the whole page.
- Ask students to reflect on the reasons for and results of their efforts. Allow younger students to reflect orally. Older students should write their reflections and use the template with three rating scales instead of coloring in three meters. The version for intermediate students has the three gauges at the top of the page and a half-page for written reflection below.

WHAT TO LOOK FOR:

- Check that the students' reflections are reasonable. If a student's estimate of effort differs greatly from yours, talk with the student.

NEXT STEPS:

- Return student work. Have students describe the connection between their effort and achievement. Students who see the relationship between their effort and achievement usually become more motivated learners.

Student Tools

TIPS/VARIATIONS:

- Use this tool with a set of assignments instead of one. For example, use it with a portfolio (as a reflection on the whole body of work).
- Allow students to work in groups so they can compare their perceptions of concentration, time, and care with the perceptions of others.
- With some modifications in instructions, use this tool to have a group reflect on their group efforts.

Effort-o-Meter

INTERMEDIATE VERSION

Assignment <u>Book Report on <u>Sarah, Plain and Tall</u></u>

Color the meters to answer the questions.

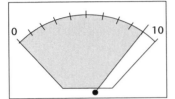
How hard did you concentrate?

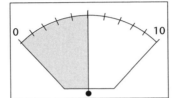
How much time did you spend?

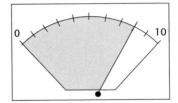
How carefully did you work?

Why did you give these ratings?

> I worked real hard on my report because I really liked the book.
>
> Writing the report didn't take as much time as I thought it would because I had a lot I wanted to say. But I was real careful, and I checked my final copy before I turned it in.

Student Tools

Effort-o-Meter

PRIMARY VERSION

Assignment _____

Draw lines on the meters. Rate your work.

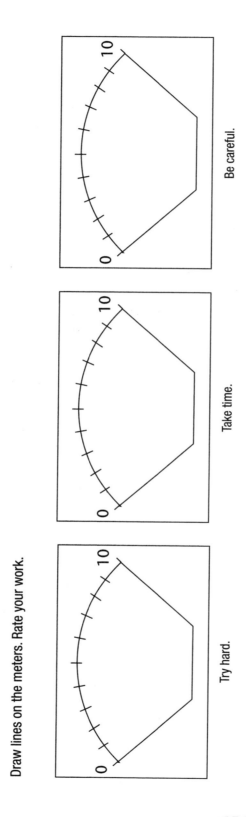

Try hard.

Take time.

Be careful.

Effort-o-Meter (*continued*)

INTERMEDIATE VERSION

Assignment _____

Color the meters to answer the questions.

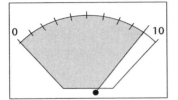

How hard did you concentrate?

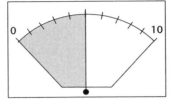

How much time did you spend?

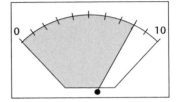

How carefully did you work?

Why did you give these ratings?

Effort-o-Meter (*continued*)

SECONDARY VERSION

Assignment _____

Rate your work on this assignment.

How hard did you concentrate when you did this assignment?
- ○ As hard as I could
- ○ A lot
- ○ Some
- ○ Not much
- ○ Not at all

How much time did you spend on this assignment?
- ○ A lot
- ○ Some
- ○ Not much
- ○ None at all

How carefully did you work on this assignment?
- ○ I did my best.
- ○ I was pretty careful.
- ○ I was somewhat careful.
- ○ I was not very careful.

Why did you give these ratings?

Student Tools

Go Over a Test

STEPS IN THE FORMATIVE ASSESSMENT PROCESS SUPPORTED BY THIS TOOL:

☑ Understand target   ☑ Evaluate strengths and weaknesses

☐ Produce work   ☑ Prescribe action for improvement

☑ Compare work with target   ☐ Take action for improvement

HOW TO USE:

- Use this tool after students have taken a test individually and the graded tests have been returned to them. Because students often experience a test as an end point after a unit is over, they may feel material is "done" and doesn't matter anymore. This tool's purpose is to help students continue to learn beyond the test.
- Use this tool with multiple-choice, true-false, matching, or short-answer (fill-in-the-blank) tests, where an answer key is available. Put the correct answers in the second column before photocopying the tool. (If the test is long, use additional sheets as necessary.)
- Have students look over their papers item by item in small groups. Instruct students to note how many group members got each item wrong, and to explain in the last column why the given correct answer is right. Tell them they may use books, notes, their own tests, and each other to do this. If no one in a group got an item wrong, group members should simply write "0" and move on.

WHAT TO LOOK FOR:

- Check that the explanations are correct and demonstrate understanding.

NEXT STEPS:

- Have students discuss what they learned and how they might use this information in the future (e.g., in other lessons, on another test).

TIPS/VARIATIONS:

- Give students another form of the same test after they have studied from the tool.

Source: From *Grading* (Fig. 6–13), by Susan M. Brookhart, 2004, Upper Saddle River, NJ: Pearson Education Inc. Used by permission of Pearson Education Inc.

Student Tools

Go Over a Test

Test _The Age of Jackson_

Group member names _Sally, Tenisha, Robert, Graham_

Look at each question on the test and then at the correct answers below. If one or more of your group members got a question wrong, note how many and then write an explanation of why the correct answer is right. You may use your book or other materials. If no one in your group got the question wrong, note a 0 (zero) and move to the next item.

Test Item	Correct Answer	Number in Your Group Who Got This Wrong	Why Is the Correct Answer Correct?
1.	B		
2.	A		
3.	B		
4.	D		
5.	C		
6.	A		
7.	A		
8.	D		
9.	B		
10.	B		
11.	A		
12.	C		
13.	C		
14.	D		
15.	B		
16.	A		
17.	D		
18	A		
19.	C		
20.	C		

This is an example of how to prepare the sheet. Students fill in columns 3 and 4 as they go over the test.

Student Tools

Go Over a Test

Test _____

Group member names _____

Look at each question on the test and then at the correct answers below. If one or more of your group members got a question wrong, note how many and then write an explanation of why the correct answer is right. You may use your book or other materials. If no one in your group got the question wrong, note a 0 (zero) and move to the next item.

Test Item	Correct Answer	Number in Your Group Who Got This Wrong	Why Is the Correct Answer Correct?
1.			
2.			
3.			
4.			
5.			
6.			
7.			
8.			
9.			
10.			
11.			
12.			
13.			
14.			
15.			
16.			
17.			
18			
19.			
20.			

Student Tools

ABOUT THE AUTHOR

Susan M. Brookhart is an independent educational consultant based in Helena, Montana, and senior research associate in the Center for Advancing the Study of Teaching and Learning in the School of Education at Duquesne University.

She is the author or coauthor of several books and many articles on classroom assessment, including ASCD's *How to Give Effective Feedback to Your Students* and *How to Assess Higher-Order Thinking Skills in Your Classroom.*

RELATED ASCD RESOURCES: FORMATIVE ASSESSMENT

At the time of publication, the following ASCD resources were available (ASCD stock numbers appear in parentheses). For up-to-date information about ASCD resources, go to www.ascd.org.

Online Courses

Visit the ASCD PD Online™ system (http://pdonline.ascd.org) to explore these and other online courses:

- Assessment: Designing Performance Assessments (#PD09OC30)
- Assessment: Measurement That's Useful (#PD09OC31)
- Assessment: Promoting Assessment for Learning (#PD09OC33)

Print Products

- *Advancing Formative Assessment in Every Classroom: A Guide for Instructional Leaders*, by Connie M. Moss and Susan M. Brookhart (#109031)
- *Checking for Understanding: Formative Assessment Techniques for Your Classroom*, by Douglas Fisher and Nancy Frey (#107023)
- *Classroom Assessment and Grading That Work*, by Robert J. Marzano (#106006)
- *Educational Leadership*, December 2007/January 2008: Informative Assessment (#108023)
- *Educational Leadership*, November 2009: Multiple Measures (#110022)
- *Enhancing Professional Practice: A Framework for Teaching*, by Charlotte Danielson (#106034)
- *Exploring Formative Assessment* (The Professional Learning Community Series), by Susan Brookhart (#109038)
- *How to Give Effective Feedback to Your Students*, by Susan M. Brookhart (#108019)
- *Improving Student Learning One Teacher at a Time*, by Jane Pollock (#107005)
- *Instruction That Measures Up: Successful Teaching in the Age of Accountability*, by W. James Popham (#108048)
- *Making Standards Useful in the Classroom*, by Robert J. Marzano and Mark W. Haystead (#108006)
- *Transformative Assessment*, by W. James Popham (#108018)
- *What Teachers Really Need to Know About Formative Assessment*, by Laura Greenstein (#110017)

Professional Interest Communities

Visit www.ascd.org/profinterestcom for information about professional educators who have formed groups around topics such as "Assessment for Learning." Look in the Professional Interest Communities Directory for current facilitators' addresses and phone numbers.

Video and DVD

- *Assessment for 21st Century Learning* (Three DVDs, each with a professional development program) (#610010)
- *Formative Assessment in Content Areas* (Three DVDs, each with a professional development program) (#609034)
- *Giving Effective Feedback to Your Students* (Three DVDs, each with a professional development program) (#609035)
- *The Power of Formative Assessment to Advance Learning* (Three DVDs with a comprehensive user guide) (#608066)

The Whole Child Initiative helps schools and communities create learning environments that allow students to be healthy, safe, engaged, supported, and challenged. To learn more about other books and resources that relate to the whole child, visit www.wholechildeducation.org.

For more information, visit us on the World Wide Web (www.ascd.org); send an e-mail message to member@ascd.org; call the ASCD Service Center (1-800-933-ASCD or 703-578-9600, then press 1); send a fax to 703-575-5400; or write to Information Services, ASCD, 1703 N. Beauregard St., Alexandria, VA 22311-1714 USA.